Child abuse and neglect, a ... has complex and imperfe ... how sometimes the system gets it right. When foster parents and faith communities step up to the plate, they can save a child.

Kathy is a good writer and has a remarkable story. So glad she is sharing it! It certainly makes a strong case for the importance of good people considering opening their hearts and homes to foster children or adoptees.

Carolyn Holderread Heggen, Ph.D.
Author of *Sexual Abuse in Christian Homes and Churches*
Sister Care Co-Presenter

Praise for *Bars, Dumps & Other Childhood Hangouts*

Everyone involved in foster care should read this first-hand account. It illuminates what goes on inside a good kid handed a difficult life through no fault of her own. The profound change foster care parents can make in a child's life is also shown, but the book's greatest impact will be in regards to enabling understanding the things foster kids may not be able to say on their own behalf. A touching story that has the potential to change lives for the better.

Stephanie Grace Whitson
Award-winning, best-selling novelist

Published by Workplay Publishing
Newton, KS 67114
workplaypublishing.com

Original cover design and interior layout by André Swartley.

Cover and interior photos provided by Katherine Burkey
Wiens. Used with permission.

ISBN 978-1-7343946-1-0

PRINTED IN THE UNITED STATES OF AMERICA

Please Don't Send Me Back

a memoir by

Katherine Burkey Wiens

Workplay Publishing

Contents

To fellow survivors of childhood trauma and abuse.
To those who support and advocate for survivors of abuse.

Preface

Dear Readers,

Thank you for choosing to read this book. I appreciate your willingness to share this part of my life journey. *Please Don't Send Me Back* chronicles the second half of my childhood, starting from age eleven. There are many references in this book to things that happened in the first ten years of my life. That story is told in my first book, *Bars, Dumps and Other Childhood Hangouts*.

If you have not read my first book some of the references in the current one may be confusing. Therefore, I'm including a brief description of *Bars, Dumps and Other Childhood Hangouts,* which has been recently revised and reprinted and is available on Amazon and many other online book sellers.

The first ten years of my life I grew up in Lincoln, NE. This was from 1959 to 1970. My biological family consisted of my mother, Josephine, my stepfather, Frank and my half brother Pat. Pat was seven years older than me. Our family lived on the margins of society. There was never enough money and rarely enough food.

Frank and Josephine were both addicted to alcohol and through most of my childhood I don't remember them working regularly. They received welfare and that's what we lived on. Frank liked to go to dumps and pick up scrap metal to sell and make extra income. We spent a lot of time in bars. Pat and I would always be with them. While Frank and Josephine drank beer or hard liquor, Pat and I would sit with them and drink sugary pop.

Because of their addictions Frank and Josephine were not good parents. They didn't care for us the way we should have been cared for. I think Josephine really wanted to be a good parent, but she just wasn't strong enough to overcome her addictions. In the first nine years of my life I lived in extreme poverty, while also suffering from neglect and sexual abuse. The primary abuser was my brother, Pat. However, after the death of my stepfather, other abusers came into my life.

In April of 1969, the day after Easter, Frank died. We had all been with him going to dumps and farmers' burn piles looking for any kind of scrap metal. Frank was out in one of these fields when he fell over dead of a massive heart attack.

After that our family really started to go downhill. Josephine started drinking even more and she was bringing men into the house. Pat was seventeen and was also drinking and brought friends home. So, as a nine and then ten-year-old child my life was becoming very unsafe. I learned quickly how to keep myself safe. This included manipulating situations as best I could to thwart the perverted sexual advances of unsafe men.

Then in the winter of 1970, Pat left because he couldn't get along with the man Josephine was living with. So now I was alone with Josephine and her live-in boyfriend. Pat was an abuser, but he also kept me safe. His leaving increased my feelings of fear and insecurity.

In the summer of 1970 Josephine went away for a weekend and left me with the managers of the trailer park where we lived. The man molested me the first night I stayed with them and the next day and evening I stayed outside and didn't go back into the house when it got dark. Fearing what awaited me in their house, I walked around the block. A neighbor lady saw my plight and let me sleep in her house that night. She called the child welfare authorities and I was taken away.

After spending five months in Cedars Children's Home in Lincoln, NE I went to live with the Burkeys on Thanksgiving weekend, 1970. They were my foster family, but soon became my forever family. Today whenever I talk about my family, I'm talking about them. *Please Don't Send Me Back* starts with my last day at Cedars Children's Home.

I would also like to share with you my approach to writing memoir. People will often say they are amazed at all the details in my book. One reader stated "I am in awe of your memory for details and feeling." In writing the first book and this book I struggled with how to share my stories. All the stories in each book took place in my young life. These are stories that have stuck in my memory for all these years. Because these memories have remained strong all my life, I know they are important. I put these stories in the books to honor not only my experiences, but my young self who survived these experiences.

These stories also illustrate the theme of the book. This theme is what foster children experience when they are placed in a home. They illustrate it's central theme, which is, even though a child is in a stable, caring foster home, the abuse and neglect from the past continues to invade the child's life.

While I have stayed true to the stories of my childhood and the theme of each book, I have added on and produced scenes and dialogue. This means all the descriptions of the scenes and words in the dialogues are not produced from exact memory. However, they are true depictions of the people and what they likely said in the story.

My writing coach, Laurie Oswald Robinson, gave me literary permission to write the story in this way. Her permission freed me to share an interesting and entertaining account of my childhood. To keep a reader reading, a story must be interesting and engaging. As a writer I want to keep you, the reader, engaged. If you are engaged with the story, the theme or message of the story is more likely to come through and help you understand the life of one foster child.

Introduction

Surviving is not the same as being fine. Surviving is beating the odds, succeeding in the face of adversity. When a person has lost everything yet endures, they must create a new life. Sometimes this means pretending everything is okay. The child in this story learned to navigate the tricky waters of being accepted into a place where she had no birthright or history, where she didn't naturally belong.

Belonging is a strange thing. When people belong, they don't realize it. It's like the air they breathe. But when a person doesn't belong, it's like fighting for each breath, not knowing if the air will last. When a person doesn't naturally belong, they learn to survive by making it look like they fit in. Trying to fit in is one way to survive in a new and different situation. Fitting in is the only thing to control. A person can do or not do things to fit in, but only the tribe decides who belongs.

How can an 11-year-old child experience extreme loss and pretend to be fine?

Her stepfather was dead, her beloved brother was gone, and the state removed her from a neglectful, alcoholic home.

Because all this happened within a short 15 months, there was no time for mourning.

To prepare for what came next, she looked ahead and knew moving forward was the only way to cope.

The new life this child would navigate was foster care. That meant pretending she was okay because nobody wants a messed-up kid. Being placed in foster care is easier if everybody thinks you're fine.

Because everything was new, she had no time to grieve her loss. This child morphed into a different person to survive. This change happened out of necessity. Feeling the immense grief would have been more than her young self could handle. This girl was strong and smart, and she adapted to the new situation so quickly everyone thought she was fine. But everyone was wrong.

Now, wearing a mask and burying the grief down deep, the girl found her way. She found her way to not only survive this new world but fit in and thrive. Her loss was enormous, but like Job in the Bible, who also lost everything, this young girl gained it all back a hundredfold. She came into this new life as a foster child and left as a beloved daughter.

This is her story. This is my story.

Chapter 1

New Family

I closed the closet door, folded the pants and put them in the brown paper grocery sack sitting on the lower bunk. This is where I had slept for the last five months. No longer did this place make me scared and nervous. Now being here was normal. My last day was uneventful, unlike the first terrifying day back in July. Being taken away from my mother and brought to a new, unknown place was one of the scariest times in my life. Fear and sadness were the only feelings that first day. Now I felt calmer.

Leaving the room, I held the sack in one hand and put the toy dog with the purse body under my arm. This toy dog had a white head with long narrow ears. The body was turquoise with a zipped back. It could hold pajamas or other secret treasures. It was dirty and old. It was a thrift store gift from my biological mom, Josephine, given three months earlier, on August 23, my 11th birthday. Now it was November 25, my last day here. I wasn't going back to my old life with Josephine. A new life was waiting for me.

I was going to a new home: a nice house on a farm with a couple that seemed to care about me.

I looked around the room which was divided in half by two rows of bunk beds against the walls and tall closets in the middle. I wasn't sad about leaving, but I was nervous about going. The workers here at Cedars Children's Home cared for me and, I believe, cared about me. But they were only here for this chapter of my life. After today I would not see any of them again. Cedars was a suitable place, but for anyone who stayed here, it was only a pit-stop on their life's journey.

I stepped into the bathroom and took my toothbrush from the cup holder hanging on the wall. I would no longer be sharing this large multi-sink, toilet, and shower room with ten other girls. That was a good thing. Going to a home with a one-sink bathroom, one toilet, and bathtub will be wonderful, I thought. However, the best thing about this bathroom was that it was always clean, unlike the filthy ones I endured while living with my biological family.

Across from the bathroom was the TV/games room. Norma was there along with other girls. She looked up, short, dark, curly hair framing her face, and her penetrating brown eyes held me in her gaze. Norma was a friend who came to Cedars shortly after I did. She slept on the top bunk of my bed. But a bunk bed was not all we shared; we were about the same age and the same size.

Norma was not mean to the others girls but would stand up for herself when needed. And, like me, she was at Cedars alone. There was no sibling or friend she could attach to and make alliances. We had made a connection, but after today I would never see her again. She had to stay while I got to go, and this created anguish for both of us.

I could see she was trying to fight back the tears. Coming toward me, we exchanged one last hug. The other girls and staff had said their goodbyes at our snack time after school.

Norma and all the other children here knew these feelings well. But leaving meant I would be with people who did not understand. Being at Cedars meant losing everything. All my possessions fit in a grocery sack. Most kids have rooms full of their possessions: gifts, photos, books, things they love and things that give them an identity. But this single sack held my life.

Now at age 11, when my life had barely started, I had to start over. These emotions were so overwhelming, I could not take them in. I mourned the loss of my entire family. It was not because they died or got killed, but because they chose alcohol over me. Even though they loved me, I was not enough. I was not good enough, talented enough or valuable enough to keep. And if you're not good enough for your family, how will you ever gain the love and acceptance of others?

So here I was on the threshold of this new life, pushing aside the sadness, grief, and loneliness. The new adults in my life would not see this part of me. They would only see sweetness and obedience, or I would stay out of their way. This was how I protected myself on the outside. On the inside, I suffered from constant headaches and stomachaches. My body took in the pain and suffering because I was powerless, in an adult-centered world, to deal with it any differently.

The most important job now was finding a place to belong. I needed to fit into my new life. I had no control over being accepted in my new family. They would be the ones to decide. Figuring out what everyone wanted was my job. If I could do that, maybe they would keep me.

Embracing Norma one last time, I was not fully aware of all these feelings. They were just raw, sad and scary emotions. And even though neither of us could name what we felt, we were feeling them together. This brought peace and comfort. But now it was time to face our futures and move on. I pulled away from Norma's hug and left.

Down the hall, I walked past the playroom for the younger girls and the clothes donation room. Last, I came to the housemother's apartment. Holding my dirty, smelly, beloved dog purse under one arm and the sack in the other, I turned left toward the stairs and went down.

My stomach hurt and my head was pounding. Hugging the toy dog close to my face, I breathed in the smell of my former life. The faint aroma of cigarette smoke comforted me but also brought tears of regret. I wanted Josephine and Pat, my biological mother and brother, to be waiting for me downstairs. I wanted them to take me away to a new, normal life, free of alcohol, abuse, neglect, and poverty. But that was not happening, and I had to embrace this new reality. Ready or not, it was time to go.

At the bottom of the stairs was the cafeteria. Supper was cooking, and it smelled good, but I was glad I wouldn't be eating there anymore. From now on I would be in a real home with food prepared for four people and not for 30 to 40 children. My last stop at Cedars was the office of Alberta, the director. Waiting for me were Floyd and Erma Burkey, my new family. Soon I would be at their home on the farm. I walked out of Cedars Children's Home in Lincoln, Nebraska, on November 25, 1970. This was the last time I would see this place for many years.

***

Leaving Cedars to go to the Burkey farm was not new. I had visited the farm several times before it became my home. It felt familar and safe, like Erma and Floyd. But this was Thanksgiving weekend, and already we were leaving the farm to drive to Kansas to meet the rest of my new family. This created excitement and curiosity along with nervousness and dread.

"Okay, I think we've got everything," Floyd said early Thanksgiving morning as he shut the trunk of the green Dodge.

We all got into the car ready for our trip to Hesston, Kansas. As we drove down the long lane, gravel crackling under the tires, I looked out the back window at the cows in their pens. I trusted Floyd and Erma would not take me anywhere that was dangerous, or where people would hurt me. Their presence softened my anxiety. Looking out the window continued to occupy my time for the first hour of travel. After that I started asking repeatedly, "Are we out of Nebraska yet?" This was my first time going out of the state. It was a new and exciting adventure.

Finally, Floyd said, "Okay, we're in Kansas now." As I looked out the window, I was a little disappointed. Kansas looked exactly like Nebraska. I thought there would be something more exciting about passing from one state to another. Now this milestone in my life was over. I went back to playing with the small Barbie doll I'd brought.

Soon I was asleep. When we got to Janet and Stan's, Floyd and Erma's daughter and son-in-law's house just south of Hesston, Erma woke me.

We walked into the farmhouse. It was old but nice. The room we walked into was full of people. For me it was full of strangers. I suddenly became shy, but Floyd coaxed me out from behind him and introduced me to everyone. They all seemed nice. No one frightened me. I could smell cigarette smoke on two people, but no one smelled of alcohol. This was a comfort.

After the introductions everyone went back to visiting or watching TV. Most of the women went into the kitchen. I followed and did a few helpful things, such as putting food on the table. Then Janet took me to another room and introduced me to the children of the family. She said I could play with them.

Marty and Jody were 9 and 6 years old, the closest to my age. The younger children, Cindy, Shelly, and Steve, were 2 and 3 years old. I was glad to be with the children. This was a place where I could relax and be myself. I didn't feel a need to please the children like I did the adults.

Finally, we ate. I sat at the kids' table, and that felt comfortable to me. The food was wonderful. Eating and having a full stomach was always a comfort for me, and that was still true with this new family. The rest of the weekend was full of more food, playing with the children, and exploring the farm. On Sunday afternoon we all said goodbye. Floyd, Erma, and I drove back to Nebraska.

***

"Come on, Kathy, time to get up. You need to eat breakfast, and then I'll take you to your new school."

Erma, my new mom, had opened the bedroom door a few inches to give me the message.

I woke up to her voice, but things were fuzzy for me. As I looked around this new bedroom, I couldn't believe this was where I lived. In some ways, it still felt like a dream.

"Come on, let's get going!" Floyd's voice boomed from the bottom of the stairs and pulled me from my happy musings. I jumped out of bed and got dressed.

Downstairs at the table, cereal and milk were waiting for me, along with a bowl and spoon. "Get your own cereal. You're not a guest here anymore," Erma said from the kitchen sink.

"Yeah, you're not a guest anymore," Floyd said with a smile, and I knew no one was mad at me. We were all trying to figure out this new situation.

Floyd got up and poked me in the side as he went to the washroom to put on his coveralls. "Have a good day at school."

An hour later, Erma and I got to the elementary school, a tall, two-story brick building. Inside we went to the office. After filling out papers and answering questions, we said goodbye.

I followed the secretary to the second floor. The dark wooden stairs creaked in the old building as we walked. The walls were made of rough plaster painted white. Walking to the end of the hall, we turned into the second-to-last room. I followed the secretary in, and she gave the teacher some papers. Then the secretary introduced me to Mrs. Moser.

"Children, your attention please," Mrs. Moser clapped

her hands. The other students stopped what they were doing and looked at her, then looked at me.

"Children we have a new student. Her name is Kathy Shorny, and she comes from Lincoln. I expect you all to be friendly and helpful to her."

Being introduced this way was not a new experience, but this time it was different. This had happened many times when I lived with my biological family and often moved from school to school. On the inside, turmoil and insecurity were still all-consuming. But gone were the dirty, second hand clothes, messy, uncombed hair and cigarette smell. Today the class saw a normal 11-year-old fifth grader, freshly bathed, hair neatly combed, with in-style clothes.

Mrs. Moser was a short, rotund, older woman. On the first impression, her face looked gruff. But I would later find out she was a caring person.

***

This first month was a time of adjustment, but I was glad to be in my new family. Christmas was coming, and like Thanksgiving, it would be a festive time. I was looking forward to it, while also feeling nervous.

The Christmas planning began as December 25 got closer. There was a lot of preparation needed to get ready for the 13 people who would be staying for several days. I helped with the cleaning and making special treats: cookies and bars. Mom even asked if there was a part of the meal I would like to be in charge of. I wanted to make Jell-O; the kind restaurants served. It was clear red Jell-O placed on a leaf of iceberg lettuce with a spoonful of whipped cream on top. Mom agreed, so we put it on the menu.

Another critical part of preparing for Christmas is buying gifts. Two weeks before Christmas, Mom and I went shopping in Lincoln. Our first stop was J.C. Penney on O Street. The warm air hit my face as we walked through the front door. It felt good against the freezing winter air from outside. The happy sounds of "Jingle Bells," "Rudolf the Red-Nosed Reindeer," and "Silent Night" drifted through the air via the overhead speakers. Decorative lights twinkled from the festive displays, and Christmas bargains were everywhere as Mom and I made our way through the crowds of other shoppers.

When living with Josephine, I had been in this store one time. That was the previous fall, and we used a clothing voucher to get a new winter coat. Now coming to Lincoln, I was on high alert, fearful of seeing people from my past. It was unlikely I would see them in this store, but I remained tense. Listening for voices from my past, the concern was that they would be drunk and make a scene. Or worse, one of Josephine's boyfriends or Pat's friends would try something with me. It terrified me that Mom and Dad would find out some awful things that happened with these men. If they knew these things, I was sure they would not want to keep me.

There was a fear of seeing my biological family, but there was also a longing. I longed to see Josephine or Pat because I missed them. I wanted to see them and talk to them, hoping that losing me would make them change. Maybe they had stopped drinking and got jobs. Perhaps if they turned their lives around, I could live with them again. But that was a long shot. Also, living with my old family would never be like my new family.

"Let's go up to the second floor," Mom said. "That's where the clothing department is. Maybe we can find something there." Her voice brought me back into the present moment and the excitement of shopping for gifts.

Mom let me choose what to give the Burkey children and their spouses: Janet and Stan, John and Brenda, Ray and Paulene, and Loree. Even though we had only met once at Thanksgiving, I wanted to get them something special, hoping these gifts would show my desire to be a part of the family. Mom let me choose what to give them, but she also provided input and guidance.

"Here are some nice sweatshirts. I think everyone would like these." Mom said.

We looked through the sweatshirts. But we soon found out there weren't enough shirts of the right color and size. Mom walked to another table and looked at more sweatshirts. But we were both disappointed, seeing these were short-sleeved.

"We don't want short sleeves. Sweatshirts are long-sleeved," I said as my face wrinkled with disgust.

"Well, let's look through these and see if we can find the right color and sizes. We need to get these gifts today. If we have to come back closer to Christmas, we'll have less choice." Mom was getting frustrated with me. Maybe she regretted the decision to let me choose gifts for the kids.

"Okay," I said, not feeling happy with these shirts.

Looking through the short-sleeved sweatshirts, I saw several colors. My thought was to get them all the same color. That would make it like we were on a team together. But Mom thought it might be better to get each couple a different color.

"Okay," I said. "That sounds like a good idea." We looked for the right colors and found the yellow sweatshirts first. This was the easiest one to figure out. Brenda loved yellow. It had been her wedding color. She and John had just been married in June.

Next, we found teal blue shirts. We decided Janet and Stan should have those. We chose orange shirts for Ray and Paulene. Then we had to choose a color for Loree and me. It was hard finding two smalls in the same color. Finally, we decided on white. These weren't the exact gifts I had hoped to get for the Burkey children, but they were okay. We had decided, and that was a relief.

***

Three days before Christmas, with most of the preparations done, Loree was coming home tonight. She was the youngest child in the family, in her early 20s. She worked and lived in Hesston. As we waited, excitement and nervousness engulfed me. We were strangers, but I hoped a special relationship was about to begin. Being sisters is a unique bond, one I had never experienced. Would this visit start that relationship?

Just before supper, lights shone through the living room window as Loree's car came down the lane.

"Floyd, she's here," Mom said as she went to the door. Dad followed her, but I stayed in the living room, not knowing what to do.

Loree, Mom, and Dad sat at the kitchen table talking. I got up and went to the kitchen, too, but no one seemed to notice me. Maybe Loree didn't care I was there. Or maybe, like me, she didn't know what to do, how to talk or relate to this person who was a stranger but now also a part of the family. As their adult conversation died down, Loree turned and asked how school was. This was always a safe question to ask a child. It broke the ice and started a conversation. That tiny opening started a new relationship between us.

The next day Loree and I worked to get ready for the rest of the family. We talked and laughed and got to know each other better. Later in the afternoon, with all the work done, Mom said we could take a break.

We tested some goodies we made. Then I asked Loree about her guitar. She played and sang and had even made an album. Having listened to it often, I was in awe of her talent.

Singing in public was something I had done, too. While living with Josephine, I sang "Harper Valley PTA" in a bar on Ninth Street in Lincoln. People in the bar had even given me money as I'd walked around the bar singing. I had dreams of becoming a singer like Loree and making an album, too.

Singing in a bar differed from the way Loree sang. Her songs were Christian. Would she see any value in the singing I had done? It might make her think I liked bars and life with Josephine more than her and my new family. I had to avoid this impression at all costs.

So that December afternoon, Loree played her guitar, and we sang together. Then we made up a song.

"What should our song be about?" I asked.

"Let's make it something about Christmas."

"Okay," I said, "but it doesn't feel like Christmas; there isn't even any snow on the ground."

"So let's sing about a brown Christmas instead of a white Christmas."

At that moment we both knew what we would sing about. We used the song "White Christmas" by Bing Crosby, but changed "white" to "brown" and made up our own words.

"*I'm dreaming of a broooown Christmas,*" Loree sang. "*Just like the ones I never knew.*"

"*Where the trees don't glisten, and children don't listen.*" We sang this line together.

"*To hear tractors as they go,*" Loree finished the line.

Then we both started laughing. And we continued laughing, tears streaming down our faces. Loree tried to pull herself together and sang again.

"*I'm dreaming of a broooown Christmas with every Christmas cookie I burn.*"

"*May your days be dreary and dull.*" Then we both broke out in laughter. After a minute we recovered.

Then we sang the last line. "*And may all your Christmases be broooown.*"

As we doubled over in laughter on the living room couch, Mom came in.

"Boy, something must be funny. But it's time to start supper. Dad will be in from choring soon, and Ray's are coming tonight. So let's get going."

The sister next to Loree in age was Paulene. She, her husband Ray, and their children were coming that evening. With more authority placed on the men in this family, the entire family unit was often referred to by the man's name. So, there were Stan's, John's, and Ray's.

The next day, Christmas Eve, Janet and her family and John and Brenda came. Now everyone was home, and the house was full. It was stressful for me to have so many new people around. I struggled with knowing what to do and how to act. Feeling most comfortable with the women and children, I helped in the kitchen and played with the children. They considered this "women's work," and because I was a female, this is where I belonged. The men in the family seldom ventured into either of these areas. Because I felt less safe with men, I was glad for the separation.

Another thing about everyone coming for Christmas was all the presents under the tree. The Christmas tree was small, and there were piles and piles of wrapped gifts under it. But opening them would have to wait until Christmas morning.

Chapter 2

Christmas 1970

I woke with two faces looking at me.

"Come on, wake up," Cindy said.

"Yeah, we want to play, and it's time to eat breakfast," Shelly said.

These were my new little nieces. They were both 3 years old, and I enjoyed being with them. However, I wanted to sleep. As an 11-year-old, sleeping late in the morning was a great joy. But sleep was also an escape. It was a way for me to be by myself and not worry about everyone else's expectations of me. But the last couple of days I had to sleep on the couch because everyone was home for Christmas, and my bedroom, and all the other bedrooms, were full.

It was easier to make myself get up when I slept on the couch in the living room, where everyone could see me. With so many people in the house, there was a lot of noise, and this always made me feel anxious. While living with Josephine, there were many people in the bars we frequented. These people were strangers, and the loud noises often meant someone was angry or about to start a fight. The sounds I heard now--dishes clanging, silverware clinking and the electric mixer running--were becoming familiar and soothing. The smells in the kitchen were also good: bread baking meat cooking and sugary desserts being prepared.

Quickly I went to the bathroom and changed from PJs to regular clothes. Today was Christmas, so I put on my favorite outfit. It had a yellow shirt with black and white pants, and straps over the shoulders. This was a stylish outfit for the early '70s, and it was very comfortable.

Stepping out of the bathroom, I heard Erma's voice. "Kathy, fold up your blanket and sheet and put it on the bed in our room. Then come and eat breakfast."

I did as she said and was soon at the table with a bowl of cereal, orange juice, and a cinnamon roll. In Erma Burkey's kitchen, children always ate their cereal and drank juice before having a cinnamon roll. The sugary, sweet roll helped calm my anxiety from the full house.

The previous year had been the first Christmas Josephine, Pat, and I had celebrated without Frank, my stepfather. He had died the previous April. We had a tree and thrift-store gifts. Josephine was vacillating between two men, John and Marvin. Marvin lived in the house, and there were always a lot of other men around, too. Most of these other men were Marvin's nephews or Pat's friends. It hadn't felt like a real Christmas because our family was not complete.

Now this Christmas was entirely new. Even though I missed Pat, Josephine, and Frank, being here with my new family was much better than being with Marvin and Pat's new friends. This place was much safer. But no one here seemed to understand that I had a different family and that I missed them this Christmas. No one asked about them, and I tried to stay busy and not think about it.

Erma's voice broke into my thoughts, "Kathy you'd better start on that red Jell-O if you want it to be ready for dinner. It will need time to set."

I got out of my chair, raced to the sink to put my dishes in the warm soapy water.

"I started the water for you," she said.

Going to the cupboard, I got out two boxes of red Jell-O and a large bowl. Carefully I poured the powdered Jell-O into the bowl, then hot water to dissolve it. The sweet, strawberry smell was delightful as the hot water mixed with the red powder. Last, I poured it into a large flat pan and put it in the fridge. It would take a few hours for the Jell-O to get firm. When the parts of the dinner that could be made ahead of time—bread, pie and cooking the potatoes—were done, it was time for the next event. Christmas presents!

Everyone was awake by then and had eaten their breakfast. Also, the men came in from doing the chores. We gathered in the living room, and all found a place to sit. Feeling excited to open my presents, I was also eager for everyone to unwrap the sweatshirts.

Before we opened Christmas presents, Floyd read the story from the Bible. Then we sang songs while Loree accompanied us on her guitar. Finally, the time came to open the gifts. The grandchildren went first. They got toys and began playing with them. Then it was my turn. All my gifts sat before me, and I opened them one by one.

Opening presents

First, I opened the gift from Floyd and Erma. Not wanting to seem greedy or wild, I carefully peeled back the paper. When the gift emerged—a small transistor radio in a green leather case—I looked at my new parents. The smile on my face echoed the joy in my heart.

"Thank you. I love it! Now I can listen to music wherever I want!"

"Well, only good music," Dad said. "None of the crazy rock stuff." He gave his parental guidance about "good music," as any Christian father would. But his delighted expression told me he was glad I liked the gift.

I loved my radio. Not only was this something I truly wanted, it showed me Mom and Dad understood what a child my age would want. Coming from a poverty-stricken family which was also controlled by alcohol, my wishes had rarely been fulfilled. This gift communicated to me that in this family understood what I liked and who

I was: a pre-teen who loved listening to music.

Other presents were a knitting loom, the book *Blue Willow* by Doris Gates, and a green hat and scarf. I enjoyed all these gifts. In the excitement of opening my presents, I forgot about my biological family and what they might be doing, just 30 miles away in Lincoln.

It was now time for "the kids" to open their presents from me—the sweatshirts.

"These are from Kathy," Mom said, when the gifts were passed out.

They opened them at the same time. As the sweatshirts emerged, everyone seemed to like them. They all said thanks and smiled at me.

"Oh, I like the color," Brenda said. Her caring smile communicated her appreciation that I'd gotten her favorite color. Later, we all put the sweatshirts on and took a picture. All the Burkey siblings were in the picture, including me. In my young 11-year-old mind, I thought having a picture together meant I belonged.

Matching sweatshirts

There were several pictures of me taken that Christmas morning. As a pre-teen, I loved pictures of myself. But this went beyond the developmental egocentrism of an 11-year-old girl. Having my picture taken meant people realized I was there, and maybe they even thought I was important. Until then the only images I had of myself were a strip of pictures taken at the Walgreens store on O Street, in Lincoln. I went alone and sat alone in the dark photo booth while an automatic camera took three pictures.

Kathy, age 10

Now in my new family, they took several pictures of me, even one with the other kids. These photos began my journey of becoming a Burkey child.

After the presents were all opened, it was time for Christmas dinner. Aside from helping set the table and putting the food on, my responsibility was to get the red Jell-O out.

I took the pan out of the fridge. Erma cleared a place for me on the kitchen table. I set it on the table, and Erma came over to supervise. With trembling hands, I picked up the metal spatula with the wooden handle. This salad was for Christmas dinner, and it had to be perfect. My stomach tightened as Erma instructed me on how to cut the Jell-O into perfectly sized pieces. I knew she would rather do this herself because it would be easier, especially if I messed it up. Plus, I believed if this Jell-O salad turned out wrong, it could spoil the beautiful, delicious, Christmas dinner everyone had worked so hard to make. Erma carefully helped me cut the Jell-O. Then I took the spatula to lift the squares out. This was the hard part, and the first one broke as I took it out. Erma said it was okay, that the first piece was always the hardest to get out. Just be careful with the rest, she advised.

The next piece was on the plate before I realized there was no lettuce under it. Oh no, another stupid mistake I thought as my whole body shook. But Erma got the lettuce leaves, we had prepared earlier, out of the fridge. Soon the process went smoothly. I laid a lettuce leaf on the plate, then carefully position the Jell-O square and put a dab of whipped cream on top.

Jody, my new niece. was there with me watching the whole thing. She wanted to help, so I told her if she was careful, she could carry the plates to the table. She carried them without dropping a single one. It pleased me that the Jell-O had turned out okay, but would everyone like it?

Soon all the food was ready and on the dining room table. We sat down to eat. The grandkids sat at the kitchen table, but I sat at the grown-up table by Loree. Floyd asked Stan to say a prayer. Usually, we had a silent prayer, but an exceptional day, like Christmas, called for an audible prayer. When Stan finished, we all dug into the food.

Everyone enjoyed the delicious meal, which was something we all had in common. There was ham, mashed potatoes, pull apart bread, butter and jelly and, of course, red Jell-O with whipped cream. To wash it down, we drank sweetened iced tea. For dessert, there was cherry pie and ice cream, with coffee for the adults.

Still nervous about messing up, I didn't know what to say or not say around the adults. I was also afraid of doing something stupid like spilling my tea or dropping a big blob of gravy on my shirt. Thankfully, that did not happen this time. I sat quietly observing what everyone one else was doing; this would help me know how to act.

There were three lessons I learned about food and eating together in this family. First, the love of food was something we all had in common. This made us a group, a family. Next, it was fun sitting around the table laughing, joking, and having serious discussions. We lingered at the table. Finally, food was a way we honored Mom. This was her domain, and she did it well. Enjoying Mom's food showed our love and respect for her.

Floyd and Erma

The last event of this Christmas day in 1970 was a play the grandkids and I performed. The story was about a poor, hungry woman who lived in a box. I played the part of the woman. As I huddled in the box, the children brought me food and blankets and said kind words. I, as the poor woman, was very grateful and thanked them. I told them God loved them, and I read a verse from the Bible.

This play served three purposes: One, it kept the children entertained. Two, it emphasized the strong faith that was the foundation of the Burkey family. An outgrowth of that faith was helping others and a strong belief in service and missions. This would be emphasized for the rest of my childhood and adult life. Even being with them for only a month, I already understood this was an essential part of the family. Because of this, the theme of the Christmas play was not about Santa Claus and elves but about the true meaning of Christmas. God gave Jesus to the world to save us, and that calls us to give to others, to care for and help those in need. This was the whole reason I was in the family. Because of their faith, Mom and Dad wanted to help children in need. This was one of the most important lessons I learned throughout my childhood with them: to love God and help others who are less fortunate.

The third purpose of this play served as a way for me to think about and remember my biological family. Even though this Christmas was good, many things reminded me of them. Several people in the family smoked cigarettes, so walking outside while they were smoking and smelling it on their clothes made me think of Josephine and Pat. I wanted to make the red Jell-O because this was what we ate at lunch with Pat when Floyd and Erma had taken me to see him in Lincoln, two weeks earlier. When Erma made the gravy, it reminded me how Josephine's gravy was often lumpy and how she hated making it.

At these times my chest and throat got tight, and I fought back the tears. If the Burkeys saw me crying because I missed Pat and Josephine, they might think I didn't like them or didn't want to be there. But that wasn't true. I felt both things. I loved being with my new family, but I deeply missed my old family. Putting on this little play about a poor, hungry woman who needed help was a way to remember Josephine without talking about her. I don't know if anyone else understood my cryptic attempt at dealing with my pain. No one mentioned it if they did.

The last big thing that happened a couple days after Christmas once again centered on food. Dad had a sensitive stomach. He was very much a meat-and-potatoes kind of guy who liked his meat and potatoes separate. We did not have casseroles at our house where the food was mixed. Spicy foods were also uncomfortable for Dad's stomach. This meant ethnic foods, even Mexican and pizza, were out.

But during this 1970 Christmas gathering, there were secretive talks about making pizza for one meal. I was not in on these discussions other than to say, Yes, I would like to have a pizza, when asked. But it concerned me because I knew making a pizza might anger Dad.

As the discussion continued through the week, there was a quiet vote being taken. Should we or shouldn't we make pizza? Was Dad's disapproval enough to stop the rest of the family from enjoying this meal? Finally, Janet, the oldest and most rebellious in standing up to Dad, decided they would make the pizza.

On one of the last evenings that we were all together Janet, Paulene, and Loree, against Dad's objections, started the pizza.

The smells coming from the kitchen were delicious. First, the rising dough smelled heavenly. Dad did not seem to mind this too much. But when the aroma of the pizza sauce with its delightful mix of spices filled the air, Dad's objections and frustrations grew. His disapproval would not thwart Janet, and she continued to lead Paulene and Loree in the pizza-making rebellion.

Soon it was time to put the pizza together and bake it. First, they flattened the dough in the pan, then the spicy sauce was spread on top. The meats, hamburger and ham came next, topped with mozzarella cheese.

For Dad, mixing these ingredients together and the smells they produced seemed more than he could handle. When his gagging sounds did not deter the merry gang of pizza makers, he took more drastic measures. He went into the bathroom, came out with a can of shaving cream and sat at the dining table. Then he took shaving cream and placed a giant blob in his palm. He attempted to diminish the smell of the pizza by smelling the shaving cream in his hand. He also tried to show everyone the torture he was experiencing because pizza, even the smell of it being made in his house, upset his stomach.

Mom and I did not help with the pizza making. We would have to live with Dad after everyone else left. And Dad had an excellent memory about the wrongs committed against him. We both, however, thoroughly enjoyed eating the pizza. I felt sorry for Dad. He really didn't like pizza, and he must have felt disrespected when everyone ignored his wishes.

Janet stood up to and argued with Dad in a way no one else in the family could. Loree and Paulene also stood up to Dad, but to a much lesser degree. John was quieter than his sisters, but he seemed to feel less of a need to stand up to Dad. As the only male child, Dad respected him more than the women and would have rarely argued with him

The pizza-making adventure was another early family lesson for me. I knew I would never be a rebel like Janet. And as a woman, I would never have Dad's respect, as John did. Also, as a foster child, my position in the family was unsure. The lesson I learned from that evening and continued to understand was that Dad was in charge, and you didn't cross him. He was the head of the family and had all the power. I learned the lesson that evening, and it would soon be reinforced.

Chapter 3

The Dark Side of Dad

On a frigid February night, children from Bellwood Mennonite church piled out of their cars to rush into the local roller rink. The girls had come in one car and the boys in the other. This segregation was not a demand from the adults but self-imposed by the youth. When children are in the fifth and sixth grades, they may want to sit with members of the opposite sex, but they don't want anyone to *know* they want to.

As our warm breath met the freezing cold, bellows of vapor poured from our mouths. We pulled our hoods and scarves around our faces and rushed the short distance from the cars to the rink. Inside the air was warm. Immediately we forgot the cold winter night as we stepped into this new world. The smell of popcorn mixed with body and foot odor did not dampen our enthusiasm. Loud music bounced off the walls and merged with the rhythmic hum of skates gliding across the floor. Tonight, we would not need to walk. We would sail around the large oval room as the lights glittered and the music blared, propelled by the strength of our legs and the four wheels connected to our feet. I had not roller-skated much, but I loved it. Now I got another chance to practice at the skating rink in Seward.

After peeling off my coat, hat, and gloves I went to the counter and got my size 5 1/2 skates. After putting them on, I stood up and immediately felt wobbly. Grabbing the posts and the railing, I wheeled myself onto the smooth skating floor.

Madge, one of my new friends, saw my unease and grabbed my hand. "Come on, let's skate! Hold my hand, I'll help you."

Soon I steadied myself and started skating on my own. I felt secure rolling straight, but as the curve came up, my body tensed. I clumsily moved my feet and made the turn.

"You're doing good. Just keep going," a familiar voice said as he passed me. Dad was a good skater and confident in his ability. The skating party was an event for the whole church, so both adults and children were there. A lot of the men and some of the women skated. Many of the church women, including my mom, brought food and set it on the tables.

I skated for a while with my friends. When our legs tired, we sat down at the tables and had a snack. Soon we were up and going again. After a while, the lights dimmed, and the announcer said it was time for a couple's skate. We all got off the floor and sat on the benches. Boys asked other girls to skate, but no one asked me.

"Kathy, come on, let's skate." I looked up and saw Dad standing in front of me.

I had hoped a boy would want to skate with me. The pastor's son was a few years older and cute, and I'd hoped he would ask me. But here was Dad inviting me to skate with him.

My body tensed as I looked up at him. Skating with a boy from church would have been fine, but I didn't know about skating with Dad. He was a man. None of the men in my life before coming to Milford had felt safe. These men only saw women and girls as being good for one thing: having sex. I didn't get that sense from Dad, but could I take the risk?

If I took his hand and skated in the dark with him, would he read something into that? Would he think I had feelings for him? Couples skating was for people who were dating. If I agreed to hold his hand in a dark place, would he think there was something more between us? And what would that mean when we got home? What might he do? Because of the sexual abuse I experienced in my biological family, my perception of relationships and physical contact with males was skewed. I felt no sexual vibes from Dad, but could I take a chance?

I looked up and said, "No thanks," then quickly looked back down to my feet. He skated away without saying a word. I didn't know what this meant. Was he mad at me, and that's why he said nothing? Or maybe it was no big deal to him. Either way, he left me and went to the food table to talk with Mom.

As I sat there watching the others skate, I saw Ellis, a middle-aged man, fall. He was holding his wife's hand, but she stayed upright. I didn't think much about it. Many people, including me, had fallen that night. But Ellis did not get up. His wife, Rosemary, took his hand and tried to help him, but as she did, he touched his leg. His eyes squeezed shut, discomfort showing in his face. Rosemary turned to the people sitting at the snack table and told them to have the lights turned up. Then she turned back and examined her husband's leg. Others went over to the couple to see if they could help. Rosemary was a nurse, so she took the lead. Ellis stayed on the floor and another man from church skated to the man working at the rink. I moved over to the adults at the snack table.

"What's wrong with Ellis? Why can't he get up?" I asked.

"I think he broke his leg. Rosemary told Larry to call the ambulance," Mom said.

I sat there in silence, not knowing what to do. We couldn't get back on the floor; we had to keep it clear for the ambulance guys. I didn't want to skate anymore, not after seeing someone fall and break his leg.

We heard the ambulance sirens, and soon the paramedics came into the building. They examined Ellis and gently lifted him onto the stretcher and carried him outside. Sitting and watching this scene, I stared ahead, my mind felt numb, my stomach felt tight. I took a Rice Krispy bar and ate it automatically. The sweetness of the sugar did not calm me as it usually did.

My thoughts went back to sirens I heard two years earlier. Frank, my stepfather, lay dead in a farmer's field, and the paramedics came, lifted him onto a stretcher and carried him to the ambulance, just like they did with Ellis. Frank was my father for the first nine years of my life, but that day he died of a heart attack. He was going to look through a farmer's burn pile for scrap metal he could sell and make a few extra bucks. Our whole family had been with him. I sat in the car and watched him fall over. Then I rode in the ambulance with Josephine as the paramedics performed CPR on him. He was pronounced dead at the hospital.

Now this accident at the skating rink in Seward brought it all back. My stomach continued to hurt, and my chest and throat got tight. Floyd and Erma knew my stepfather died, but they didn't know the details. I didn't feel I could tell them. So I sat there staring, feeling numb, as everyone else was moving around me, taking off skates and getting their coats on.

"Kathy, you need to take your skates back to the counter. Didn't you hear me? Now finish that Rice Krispy bar and get moving."

I looked up and saw Erma standing by me. I quickly did what she asked. By then our two hours were up. They packed away the food, and it was time to go home. I rode home with Mom and Dad rather than carpooling back to the church. Our farm was between Seward, where the skating rink was, and the church in Milford, so it made sense to just go home.

The night started out fun but ended with sadness. One sad thing was Ellis' broken leg. This would disrupt his life and his family. There would be pain and recovery. Being on crutches in the cold, snowy Nebraska winter would not be fun either. This was the public, visible sad event that had occurred that evening. But there was also a personal and deep sadness that occurred. I felt the pain of my past; my stepfather's death came back. This was my silent pain.

Little did I know Floyd also suffered in silence at the skating party. It deeply hurt him when I turned down his invitation to skate. I also did not know how his pain would boomerang back to hurt me in the next couple of weeks.

Leaving the skating rink, Erma, Floyd, and I got in the car. Floyd slammed the car door when he got in and said nothing on the drive home. I could tell he was mad, but I didn't know why or who he was mad at. He said nothing, but in the next couple of weeks, his actions were more than simply passive-aggressive. He did not speak to me or look at me and acted as if I did not exist. One example of this is when we went to the cafe for dinner the next Sunday and I walked in behind him. Rather than holding the door so I could catch it, so it would not slam shut on me, he let the door go as if I was not even there walking behind him.

This went on for a week or more. It seemed like a mean, painful eternity. From an emotional standpoint, I didn't know if I would live or die. Would he treat me this way forever? Or would it be worse, would he send me back to Cedars? Then what would happen? He had all the power and as a foster child in his care; I was powerless. The only thing I could control was my ability to please and try to keep him happy.

After a while, things got better, and eventually he was nice again. However, we never talked about it. Dad was so focused on himself and his own pain he never realized the hell he put me through.

Even though Dad was often self-absorbed, he was a good man who longed to serve God and care for his family. As with all people, his life was a product of his environment and upbringing. The childhood Dad experienced in the 1920s and '30s in rural Nebraska was difficult. His mother died when he was 2 years old. His grandmother and aunts stepped in and took care of him, but this loss of such an important relationship at a critical time in his development likely changed the way he viewed and related to women as an adult. Not long after his mother died, his father remarried, so Dad had a new stepmother.

Many family members say Sarah Burkholder Burkey was a kind and caring woman, but my dad never seemed to connect with or feel the loving presence of a mom from her. The family expanded with new half-siblings. As is often the case in blended families, Dad felt his stepmother favored her biological children over him and his brother.

Because Dad's generation was one of "don't show emotion," "pull yourself up by your bootstraps" and move on, he never seemed to resolve the issues of the hurt little boy whose beloved mother died and who never connected with or felt loved by his stepmother. This produced several repercussions in Dad's adult life. First, he cared about children who needed help. He and Mom helped many children over the years. This was a big part of why they took me in as a foster child. This early pain also caused anger that would come out in outbursts or in silent treatment.

So, on that cold winter night at the skating party, when he opened himself up by asking me to skate and I said no, he was deeply hurt. This likely caused his unkind actions toward me. And because he was so angry and had ultimate power over me, I could never tell him why I said no to his invitation to skate.

Dad's actions provided powerful lessons for me. First,

if I ever had any doubt about who was in control, I didn't after this experience. Dad had all the power. This was probably his conscious goal, to exert his parental power and control and make me an obedient child. This is the goal of many authoritarian, "spare the rod, spoil the child" parents: obedience at all costs.

The other powerful way this situation affected me was the sense of abandonment I felt from Dad. His ignoring and treating me as if I wasn't there was emotional abandonment. In the previous two years, my entire biological family had abandoned me. My stepfather Frank died, my brother Pat left the family, and Josephine allowed the state to take me from her. I could not risk more abandonment in this new family. Dad's response also told me that if I did not do what he wanted, he could easily abandon me, too. He did it emotionally in those couple of weeks, and I didn't believe it would be hard for him to abandon me physically by sending me back to Cedars. Surviving meant staying in this family, and I would do what it took to stay with them. That meant being obedient and submissive to Dad.

Chapter 4

Talking to the Judge

Even though Dad did not do a good job of protecting me from himself, he was protective of me from the outside world. Mainly he wanted to keep me safe from my past life. This was one way he showed his love for me. This came through in the next big event I experienced as a foster child.

"Tomorrow is the big day," Dad said as we sat at the kitchen table.

I looked down at my Wheaties, floating in a pond of milk with banana islands dotting the surface.

"Aha," was all I said.

This was a typical weekday morning. Mom, Dad, and I sat around the kitchen table eating breakfast. This was usually a pleasant beginning to the day. Ordinarily I enjoyed the smell of coffee, bacon, eggs, and toast popping out of the toaster. Today my senses didn't pick up any of it. A dull and numb feeling engulfed me as if I was sitting in a dark cloud.

"What dress do you want to wear?" Mom asked.

Shrugging my shoulders, I said, "Don't care."

"I think the pleated maroon dress would be good. You need to wear a dress, not pants. This is an important appointment and you need to look good," Mom said.

"Oh, Erm, who cares what she wears. It's important what she says," Dad responded.

"Well I know that, but she needs to look good, too. We want them to know we're taking good care of her."

"Oh, they'll know we're taking good care of her. But they need to know she wants to stay with us. That's the most important thing."

Mom and Dad were only talking to each other as if I weren't there. This made the gray cloud even heavier. I was causing a problem again, another disagreement between Mom and Dad. They bickered back and forth like this for a few minutes, then Dad said to me, "What are you going to tell the judge tomorrow?"

"I don't know," I said, still looking at my cereal.

I didn't know what to say. There always seemed to be a right and a wrong thing to say, and I wanted to say the right thing. But I didn't know what that was. I needed Mom and Dad to tell me what to say. I wanted to stay living here on the farm with them. But I didn't want to reject Josephine and have her out of my life. This was a huge decision, and I didn't know what to do.

"The main thing is to tell the judge you want to live with us," Dad said.

"Oh," Mom said as she suddenly realized it was almost 7:30. "Kathy, the bus will be here soon. Are you ready to go?"

"I have to get my books ready." I quickly got up and took my cereal bowl and toast plate to the sink.

That day at school it was hard to focus on my studies. I was constantly thinking about going to court and seeing Josephine. Midmorning I sat with four other fifth graders around a table in the library, but it was as if I was a million miles away. I didn't feel the wooden seat of the chair or my feet on the floor.

"Kathy, it's your turn to read," said the girl sitting next to me said, nudging me with her elbow. I looked at her, and she pointed to the next paragraph. Slowly my lips moved. During lunch, I barely touched my food. Even my favorite chocolate pudding held no appeal.

At supper that night, we talked again about going to court. During this conversation, I got up the courage to ask Mom and Dad what to say. They gave me a simple answer; just tell the judge you want to stay living here. This was a good thing for me, since it helped me sleep better that night.

The next morning, we ate breakfast and drove to Lincoln. We arrived at a huge white building and found a space in the parking lot. This building was in downtown Lincoln, and I had seen it many times. During the last year living with Josephine, after Frank died, I had been in downtown Lincoln a lot. There were several bars she liked to go to in this area. Sometimes we would get a ride with someone else, but many times we had to walk, so I knew this area well.

I had seen the courthouse often, but I hadn't been inside. I did not understand what it was. Now I knew this was the judge's building. Here I'd see Josephine again and say I didn't want to live with her. With this thought, my stomach hurt so much I had to close my eyes and hold my breath. I was glad Mom and Dad were there with me as we went into the building and up the elevator, but their presence was not enough to take away my fear.

Mom and Dad worked together to navigate which floor we needed, then down the hallway to the right room. We walked into a room with several chairs lining the walls. There was another room right beside the first, separated by glass walls. This room had a large desk in it. A woman was sitting behind the desk typing on a typewriter. She looked up when we came in.

Mom and Dad told her who we were, and she directed us to two large doors on the other side of the room. Dad took my hand, and we walked through the doors. Inside was a large room, but it was not what I expected. I thought going to see the judge meant a big courtroom with a man sitting up high and wearing a black robe, like the TV show Perry Mason. This was a regular room with a large table in the middle. Several people sat around the table. I didn't look at anyone. I kept my head down and sat where Dad told me. I sat between Dad and an empty chair. I wondered who would sit there.

I also wondered where the judge was. He must not be here yet because no one wore a black robe. And where was Josephine? My stomach felt tight again. No one told me what would happen. Silently I sat, only moving my toes in my shoes. This way everyone would think I was okay, and no one would know how scared I was.

Next, the door behind me opened, and Josephine came in. She smiled and gave me a big hug. The smell was familiar—cigarettes and beer—but her embrace felt good. Her unique scent competed with the sweet fragrance of Dad's aftershave. This made my stomach feel queasy and my head hurt.

After Josephine sat down, the person sitting directly across from me cleared his throat, and everyone got quiet. Maybe he was the judge. Shouldn't he have banged a little wooden hammer to get "order in the court"? But there was no wooden hammer and no black robe. None of this was what I expected.

The grownups went around the room and said their names. Some of them smiled at me. The man sitting directly across from me read from the papers in front of him. He was saying things I really didn't understand. This was mostly because I was so nervous and scared. I was nervous because Mom and Dad were on one side of me and Josephine was on the other, I felt split between the two. Would I really be able to say what Mom and Dad had told me to say?

"Okay Kathy, now we need to hear from you." The judge's words brought me out of my thoughts, but I didn't respond.

"We've heard from all these other people about what they think would be best for you. Mr. and Mrs. Burkey have said they'd like to have you stay in their home, but you're old enough to tell us what you want."

I froze.

I knew I should say something, but the words would not come. Finally, the judge broke the silence.

"What grade are you in, Kathy," he asked in a calm, relaxed voice.

This was an easy question to answer. The fifth grade," I said.

"And you go to Milford schools?"

"Yes"

"What's the name of your teacher?"

The judge continued to ask these questions about my school, my church, and living on the farm.

I was feeling relaxed and answered more easily when the judge asked how I liked living with Mom and Dad.

"It's good," I said, looking at Mom and Dad and smiling.

"So what was it like when you lived with your mom in Lincoln?" the judge said, then smiled and asked, "Was that always good?"

I looked down at the table. I said nothing, but I shook my head no.

"Kathy, we're all here today to figure out what's best for you. We have to decide where would be the best place for you to live. Do you think going back to live with your mom would be best for you or living with the Burkeys on their farm?"

The judge stopped talking, and there was silence in the room. Under the table, I felt Dad take my hand and give it a squeeze. This simple action gave me the courage to say what I needed to say.

I turned and looked at Josephine. She was already looking at me. "Mom, I think it would be best if I stayed with them," I said, pointing to Floyd and Erma.

Josephine looked sad rather than angry. She was an emotional person, sometimes screaming at the top of her lungs, usually to Frank or later to Marvin. At other times she burst into tears at the drop of a hat. Now I couldn't read her expression, except I knew she was sad. In the past, her extreme emotions had been how she expressed power. Maybe she realized she couldn't do anything in this situation, so she nodded and looked away.

The truth was the judge had helped me say why living with Mom and Dad was much better for me. Through his questioning about my new life, I could say how much happier I was and how this life was much more stable than living with Josephine. He helped pave the way for me to give the answer I wanted. He gave me the ability to turn away from my old life with Josephine and toward my new one.

"For the record, Kathy, tell me what you want. Do you want to live with the Burkeys or with your mom?"

"The Burkeys," I whispered as I stared at the table.

This was the end of the meeting. They passed papers around for everyone to sign. I signed my name along with the adults. Then we all got up and went out of the room.

Mom and Dad stopped to talk with a woman who had been in the meeting. This left a little space for Josephine and me to speak privately. I thought she would talk about what had just happened or maybe tell me where Pat was and what he was doing. But she didn't say either of these things.

"Do you want to call Marvin 'Marvin' or 'Daddy Marvin'?" she said. As we stood in the office waiting room, with only a few minutes alone, this is the question she asked me.

I stood and looked at her. "I don't care," I said.

Then I had nothing more to say. This question was

so bizarre. Josephine asked nothing about my life. I told the judge I wanted to live with the Burkeys, but it didn't seem to faze her. This short conversation was strange, and I could feel the distance between us becoming more significant.

Then I felt a hand on my shoulder. "Come on, Kathy, it's time to go." Dad's voice came from behind me.

I turned and saw both Mom and Dad there. I said okay and gave Josephine a hug. She held on, and I was the one that pulled away first, not wanting Mom or Dad to think I wanted to stay with Josephine or had changed my mind from what I told the judge.

Mom, Dad, and I walked out of the judge's office and back through the building the same way we came in. When we got in the elevator, my stomach became less tight and stressed. I was glad this was over. But I also felt a pang of immense sadness. Even though all this was good and what I wanted, I also wanted Josephine in my life.

There was also another question. Did Josephine want me in her life? She didn't fight that day. So often, in my childhood, I saw her put her fingers in her ears and scream, or just shout at Frank when they were angry with one another. But today she didn't resist. And then in the hall, she asked me that stupid question. I didn't want her to make a scene, but I didn't want her to let me go so quickly either.

An unconscious seed was planted that day. This seed, planted in my psyche, caused me to believe that if my mother didn't love me enough to keep me, how could anyone else ever love me? This profound lie, which I believed as truth, cemented the belief that I had to be the best I could be. That what I wanted wasn't important because I had to be perfect and please everyone. This was the only way there may be a glimmer of hope that people would not reject me.

Even though I felt I had to please everyone, I still had the basic needs of all people, especially all children. I needed love, safety, and the feeling of being valued. I enjoyed my new life with Mom, Dad, my new family, friends, and church. It was more than I ever thought I would have in my life. That instinct to survive, to find goodness and security in life had always been my driving force, both with Josephine and now with the Burkeys. If trying to be perfect and please everyone was the way to fill this need, then that's what I would do.

Chapter 5

Biking

Going to court and telling a judge you no longer want to live with your biological mother is not a typical part of childhood. There were many things about my childhood that were not typical. There was sexual abuse, neglect, abandonment, and extreme poverty. And that was only in the first 10 years of my life. Now for the second half of my childhood, I was living in a stable home with all my physical needs met. And the adults who cared for me did not have addiction issues.

So my new home was safe, but my *place* in this home did not feel secure. And I felt a constant need to hide my differentness. I wanted to belong in this new family so desperately that I hid anything that made me look or seem different.

There are many things kids who grow up in typical families experience without thinking about them. Things like health care, dental care, adequate amounts of food and clothing. These were things I didn't always have in my biological family. And there were other things I had not learned by age 11 that many children already knew how to do, like riding a bike.

I had arrived at the farm at the beginning of winter, so it wasn't until spring that I began to explore the place. When school was out in May, I looked through the garage, the machine shed, and other buildings on the farm. The old white garage was right by the old house, and that's where I found it: an old, black bike that was just my size.

At supper one evening, I asked the folks about it.

"I found an old bike in the garage. Whose bike is it?"

"Oh, I don't know, I think all the kids used it," Dad said.

"It's just a bike that's been there for a long time," Mom said.

"That thing is old. Does it still work?" Dad wondered.

"It seems to be okay," I said.

"Well, you can ride it if you want," Mom said.

Ride it, I thought. *Yes, I would love to ride it*. But the truth was I never learned to ride a bike. When I lived with Josephine, I didn't have a bike. Here on the farm, there was a bike for me, but I didn't know how to ride it.

I knew from Dad's response he thought I knew how to ride. I was eleven years old, and I'm sure in his mind all eleven-year-olds knew how to ride a bike. Kids from ordinary families learn to do this early in life, at age 6 or 7, with training wheels. But I had not come from an average family.

"The tires are flat," I said.

"You can pump them up with the air hose."

I hoped Dad would help me with this. But he must

have thought I knew how to put air in tires, too.

I did nothing with the bike for a while. I was embarrassed someone would find out my secret. This would be another way to let them know I didn't belong here. I had to figure out by myself how to do something simple, something most kids my age knew how to do. If I could master this, they might not realize how abnormal I was.

After thinking about how to teach myself how to ride a bike, the answer finally came. There was a large silage bunker in the southeast corner of the farm, right by the train tracks. This was a large concrete structure with three walls, about ten feet tall, with no top. Usually, it was full of silage, feed for the cattle, but in the summer, it was almost empty because they used the feed during the winter and spring. Now, this structure would be my training ground.

One day in early July, when no one was around, I took the old black bike and filled the tires with air. I had seen Dad put air in the car tires before, so I knew what to do. But doing it right was a different story. I wheeled the bike to the air hose and attempted to attach the nozzle to the tire. I couldn't get a good seal, so instead of putting air in I was letting it out. Finally, I got it right, and the tires were ready to go.

I walked the bike to the back of the farm, where the empty bunker stood. Looking at the ample space, I tried to figure out how to do this. Gathering up my courage, I began.

Leaning the bike up against the hard, concrete wall, I got on. Both the bike and I were standing straight up, and I put my hand on the bunker wall so I could balance.

Then I slowly put my feet on the pedals. Keeping my hand on the wall for balance, I paused again to figure out what to do next. The next step was getting my feet moving on the pedals. I did this slowly, taking one rotation of the pedals at a time. Then I paused, took my feet off the pedals, and balanced myself. I continued this way until I got to the other end of the bunker, about 30 feet away from the where I started.

This process seemed to be working, so I continued on the two other sides. I spent most of the afternoon circling the empty bunker, trying to get my balance, trying to not fall. As a healthy 11-year-old, I knew I could physically ride a bike. But emotionally I still had a lot of fear—fear of falling, yes, but also fear of failing to learn something that was normal and common for most people. Failure would only reinforce my belief I was not normal.

The time came when I could balance myself and ride around the bunker without holding onto the wall. Now it seemed easy. As I made the final pass around the bunker, I let out a joyous scream as the summer sun kissed my face. Finally, I knew how to ride a bike. Leaving the silage bunker, I rode the old black bike with new confidence. I had a new faith and trust in myself. This simple skill put me one step closer to feeling like I could fit into my new family, that I could be normal.

Chapter 6

The Purple Nightgown

Nearing my fourth Christmas with the Burkeys, life was becoming normal, but I could not shake the fear of not belonging, of being rejected by the family. Along with this fear was the need to process the grief, loss, and trauma I experienced living with Josephine and being taken away from her. I could not predict what would bring up the pain and trauma from the past. Even things that Mom and Dad meant as loving and caring gestures could trigger my young traumatized mind.

It was Tuesday, December 25, 1973. We were now living in a new house. The old house where I first came to live with Mom and Dad had been torn down, and this was our first Christmas in the newly built house.

The house was full. The noise level was high, with children running and playing, adults talking and laughing. The aroma of coffee and the sweet smell of cinnamon rolls lingered in the air all morning, and soon came the meaty smells of Christmas dinner, of turkey, dressing, and mashed potatoes.

During the space between breakfast and dinner, the family gathered around the fireplace. The children sat on the stone seat, part of the massive white brick fireplace. The adults sat on the couch, the floor, or chairs carried in from the dining room. No one sat in the recliner next to the sofa. The only person that occupied that space was Dad.

"Okay, girls, these gifts are from Grandma and Grandpa. Open them together." I held my gift and opened it along with the other girls, even though I wasn't really one of the "grandchildren." I had a unique place in the family that often felt like uncertain. Many times, it seemed like I didn't fit. Like today, I was a foster child of Mom and Dad, but I was opening gifts mainly designated for their grandchildren.

As we tore open wrapping paper and opened the boxes beneath, the room filled with *oohs* and *aahs*. Beautiful nightgowns emerged with a see-through dark purple material hanging over a solid pink lining. They covered the entire body and legs, with long sleeves and lace around around a high neck.

"Hold it up," Janet said to Jody, her oldest daughter. "Let me take a picture. Grandma made it. Isn't it beautiful?"

Mom had been taking sewing classes at the fabric shop in Seward. She had always sewn clothes, but these classes were something fun she did for herself instead of economic necessity. She learned to make underwear and nightgowns with silky knit fabrics. It gave Mom pleasure, so she used this new talent to make us Christmas gifts.

We examined the nightgowns, and everyone said how beautiful they were. I wanted to be excited about this gift too, but my stomach tightened, and my head hurt.

"Go put them on, girls, and we'll take a picture," Dad said.

The little girls picked up their new gifts and ran back to my bedroom. Following them, my anxiety was rising. I wanted to appreciate the work Mom had put into this project. Rejecting this gift would reject Mom. Making me a nightgown along with the other girls was a way to include me as part of the family. If she hadn't made me a nightgown, I would have felt left out.

In my bedroom, the little girls freely took off their clothes, with only their underwear left on, and slid the beautiful purple nightgowns over their heads and pushed their arms in the sleeves. I helped them button up the back before they ran back to the living room. Staying in my room alone, something inside me said to not take my clothes off and put on this nightgown and walk into a room full of people. Maybe putting it over my clothes would be good enough. However, the gown was not big enough to fit over my bulky winter sweater and jeans.

"Come on, Kathy, we're waiting to take the picture" came a voice from the living room.

Slowly, I walked out of my bedroom and down the hall to the living room, where everyone was waiting.

Dad asked, "Why don't you have your nightgown on? We're ready to take a picture."

"I don't want to."

"Everyone else put theirs on," he shot back. "Well, it's too late now."

Walking over to the white brick fireplace I stood in line with the others. But why should I be in the picture if I wasn't wearing the nightgown?

"Kathy, just hold it up over you, that way we can see it at least," Janet said.

I held the nightgown up and Jody, who stood behind me, held it for me so I could put my arms down and hold the sleeves. Dad took a picture. It looked silly and I could tell I had frustrated the grownups, especially Mom and Dad. But I couldn't tell them why I hadn't put on the nightgown. The truth was, I didn't understand myself. I just had a sense that it wasn't safe. Wearing the nightie with only my bra and panties underneath felt inappropriate. And parading around a group of adults, especially the men, was unsafe.

Purple nightgown

The nightie's material also bothered me. The purple see-through fabric that hung over the solid slinky cloth felt too sexy. In my biological home with Josephine, Playboy magazines lay around the house. Her boyfriends brought them in. The magazines featured pictures of women who were often wearing see-through, sexy nighties over their naked bodies. Even though this nightgown was not see-through, the material still made me uncomfortable. I mostly felt safe with the men in the family, but in my young, traumatized mind, putting on that beautiful purple nightie with the see-through material was not safe around any man.

The men in my biological family didn't need a reason to do bad stuff to me, they just did it. As a young girl, I was still fairly egocentric and thought everything reflected on me and what I did. Now, living in this new family with safer men, I didn't want to do anything that might bring on their sexual advances. If I put on the nightie and something happened with one of them, it would be my fault. This was the reasoning in my traumatized mind.

The grownups probably thought I was a stubborn, ungrateful teenager. They did not punish me for my behavior. My penalty was how embarrassed I felt, plus Mom and Dad's disapproval. But I was trying to keep myself safe. Mom and Dad often misunderstood these actions.

However, Mom and Dad were also doing what they could to protect me. When they felt a situation was unsafe, they did what they could to keep me safe. But, no matter how much we all tried, there were things from my past none of us could avoid.

Chapter 7

The Visit

I think I love you
So what am I so afraid of?
I'm afraid that I'm not sure of
A love there is no cure for.

Melody and I stood in front of the mirror in my bedroom. Hairbrushes became microphones as we sang along with the radio. This was one of my favorite David Cassidy songs. We'd look at ourselves in the mirror and then back to each other as our bodies bobbed and twisted to the beat of the music.

When the song ended, we put the hairbrushes down and laughed at the pure joy of the moment. Here we were, two friends, with the whole afternoon ahead of us. Because it was Sunday and because I had a friend over, there would be no chores to do. The biblical day of rest meant a day of freedom for children. Having company over was a sacred responsibility in our house. When company came, the focus was on them, not on the work.

"I'm hungry," Melody said. The smells of Sunday dinner—pot roast, carrots, and potatoes seasoned with onions and garlic--still lingered in the air.

"Me too," I said.

I opened the door, and we both started for the kitchen. My bedroom was in the back part of the house, so we walked past several rooms to get to the kitchen. Passing the den, I saw Mom sitting on the small couch with her feet up and shoes off. The current issue of Gospel Herald, a Mennonite magazine, lay on her lap. But her head hung down, and her eyes were closed, a Sunday afternoon nap overtaking her. As we walked through the living room, Dad was also taking a nap. His slumber was not as quiet as Mom's. His snoring competed with the football game blaring from the T.V. Melody and I tiptoed past his recliner into the kitchen.

We got the frozen Butterfinger ice cream dessert with the graham cracker crust, from the freezer. Quietly cutting two pieces, we put them on plates. Then we poured two glasses of iced tea.

"Let's go downstairs and see what's on T.V.," I whispered. Melody nodded her agreement, and we started down.

We turned on the T.V. but found everything was boring. In the 1970s, we were at the mercy of the three networks, NBC, ABC, and CBS, plus the public T.V. channel. There were no VCRs or DVD players to play movies. Computers were still huge machines only used by large companies. Desktop computers or laptops that streamed hundreds of T.V. shows or movies were just a seed of an idea in the minds of young people the same age as Melody and me.

We surfed the four channels and soon realized only sports and a PBS documentary was on. Turning off the T.V., we talked. This was always a favorite pastime for us. It was delightful to have a friend with whom I could comfortably talk to about anything. I was fortunate that Melody was here that afternoon. I would need her help for what was about to happen.

After being in the basement for a while, our snack eaten with only crumbs on the dirty plates, the doorbell rang. I looked at the wall clock, 4:00. Who was coming to visit this early on a Sunday afternoon? Everyone knew this was prime nap time, and neighbors around here would not rudely disrupt that unless it was an emergency or something important. Maybe Melody's parents were coming to pick her up early. We had planned to take her to church with us that evening, but maybe something came up, and they needed to get her now.

We heard talking upstairs. Dad called down to the basement. "Kathy, there's someone here to see you."

Who would be here to see me, I wondered?

"I hope it's not my parents coming to get me," Melody said. "We still have a few hours before church, and I wanted to stay with you."

"I know. Me too," I replied.

As we walked up the steps, I smelled something strange. It was cigarette smoke, but I knew it wasn't Dad's. The smell was too heavy to be from the little cigars he smoked, and besides, he never smoked in the house. Mom refused to let him do that. Then my senses detected more smells, body odor and alcohol. My feet continued to move up the steps, but my mind froze. I didn't want to accept who I believed was at my new house, invading my new life.

At the top of the stairs, I saw them. Immediately my stomach tightened, and I was afraid I might be sick. Fear, sadness, anger, confusion, embarrassment, and joy flooded my senses, and I didn't know how to respond to these overwhelming emotions. Finally, fear came to the surface.

"Oh Kathy, sweetheart, it's so good to see you," Josephine said as she came over and gave me a hug.

"Hi, Mom," I said in a small voice.

I wanted to look at Dad and Mom to see if they were okay with Josephine being here. Instead, I hung my head and looked at the floor. Then I pulled away from her embrace. Mom and Dad would not be happy about the other people who came with Josephine. Marvin, Josephine's boyfriend, and George, Marvin's nephew. And I knew they would not be happy that she and these men had come with no warning.

I didn't look at Melody either. Even though she was someone I trusted and could later talk to about the situation, it embarrassed me to have her see this part of my life. I wanted no one to know what I had come from, what I had been. But now, in full view, were these dirty, smelly, alcoholic people that were my family. Well, at least Josephine was. Would Melody still want to be my friend after she saw all this?

The silence in the room spoke volumes about my two worlds. Fear filled my entire body, and anger seemed to come from everyone in the room. Would Melody reject me when she found out who I really was? Would Mom and Dad's anger with this situation make them realize I was too much of a hassle and send me back to Cedars? Worst of all, Josephine, Marvin, and George now knew where I lived. They could come here anytime and do anything.

"Come and sit down," Dad said as he pointed to the living room.

Marvin, George, and Josephine sat on the green couch. I sat in the brown wooden chair next to Josephine. The chair was one I really liked, and I didn't want them sitting in it. It was part of the new living room furniture Mom and Dad bought for the new house. The chair was made of dark wood, with rounded cane side panels and soft velvet upholstery. Now, these smelly, dirty people sat on the beautiful new furniture. Dad sat in the orange swivel chair in the corner, and Mom and Melody carried chairs from the dining room table.

"So where is Pat today?" Mom asked Josephine. She knew Pat because we went out to lunch with him and his new wife, Mary, soon after I came to live with them.

"Oh, I don't see him too much. He's got his wife, and they don't have much to do with us." But what Mom didn't know was that Marvin had driven Pat away with a butcher knife in the winter of 1970. This caused us to run away to Aunt Dona's, and after that Pat didn't come home. But this was another thing I could not share with Mom and Dad. This was part of my old life, and I needed to put that aside to fit into my new life. I worked so hard at forming this new identity so I could fit in. But now all that work was being destroyed. Mom, Dad, and Melody knew who I really was and where I came from.

"What about Aunt Dona, Debbie, and Steve? Have you seen them lately?" I asked. These were my aunt and cousins, a part of my old life I really cared about. I also wanted to know about Pat. Part of me was happy Josephine came to visit. I still wanted to know about some members of my biological family.

"Oh, I don't see much of them either," Josephine said. There was silence, then Mom spoke up. "Kathy's doing really well in school. She's part of the pep club, and she goes to the youth group at church. She's made a lot of friends here."

Josephine smiled one of her big toothy grins. "Oh yes, she's always done good in school." Then she turned and looked at me. "Kathy, we're still living in the same trailer, and we got a new puppy."

"Yeah, some guy was giving them away on my garbage route," Marvin spoke for the first time. "He's real cute, brown with white stripes."

"Oh yes, he's a sweetie," Josephine added. "Maybe you can come and see him when you visit us."

Immediately I looked at Dad. He didn't say anything, but he was squeezing his lips together as his chest rose and fell in a deep breath. I could see he was getting angry. This may not have been noticeable to anyone else. But I knew. Having lived with the volatile feelings he often expressed, I didn't need to read his emotions; I sensed them. Not knowing how angry Dad might get made me feel scared. I was also afraid about what I might have to do. Would I have to go visit them in Lincoln, to the trailer where we lived? Would I have to go alone? I didn't think Mom or Dad would ever come there with me.

"I don't know if Kathy will come and visit you. The social worker will decide about that," Dad told Josephine.

"She should be able to come and see me. She's my daughter, and it is her home," Josephine replied.

Dad looked right at Josephine, his face as hard as a stone. Now everyone could see his anger. He said something, but Mom interrupted him. "Floyd, why don't you take Kathy and her family around the house, and I'll make coffee."

No, no, no, I thought. "They are not my family. Don't call them my family. I want you to be my family, not them." These thoughts screamed in my mind. But they were my family. That was the horrible truth staring me in the face.

I was still living in both worlds. I must keep my love for Josephine and Pat secret from Mom and Dad. I was trying so hard to belong and gain acceptance in my new family. Expressing my love for Josephine and Pat would only prove that I didn't fit in, didn't belong, and that I wasn't really a part of this family.

I also hated that Josephine brought these men with her, especially George. He was a man 10 years older than me. When all this craziness started, after my stepfather Frank died, and Marvin came into the picture, George came around. He was Pat's friend, and Marvin's nephew, and my "boyfriend," if that's what you call a 20-year-old man being attracted to a 10-year-old child. The reality was he was a sexual predator who had groomed and then sexually assaulted me multiple times.

Now he was invading my new life. Now he knew where I lived. I felt afraid, embarrassed and ashamed all at the same time. My mind raced with these thoughts as Dad and I showed the group the basement. The storage/storm room was the last room on the house tour. It was at the back of the basement, with concrete walls and no windows. It was the place to go if there was a tornado. One side of the room was for storage. Mom kept all her canned green beans, peaches, pears, cherries, and even canned beef on the shelves. This was the harvest of the garden, and it would supply our family with food during the winter.

After they built the house and before we moved everything in, Mom let me paint this room anyway I wanted. I chose lime green, orange, and yellow for the colors. I painted each cinder block a different color, but I kept it balanced and in a pattern. There was an old couch against the multicolored wall where I kept my stuffed animals and dolls. I enjoyed playing school in this room. I was the teacher, and the dolls and stuffed animals were the students.

This afternoon, we all crowded into the small room. As we left, I was the last to come out, and George stood there waiting for me. He looked at me with a sly smile and said in a quiet voice, "Maybe we can go in there and play house sometime."

I knew what he meant. He still wanted to get me alone and abuse me, maybe even worse than he had done before. Moving away from him, I quickly went upstairs. It was good to be out of the basement and in the living room with everyone else. This was my new world; this was where I wanted to be. I wanted Josephine to change, but I never wanted to go back to that world. All there was in my old world were men like George, lazy alcoholics who didn't work and who used women for their own pleasure whenever they could.

Now there were new men in my life who wouldn't treat me that way. Men I didn't fear. There were safe men at church and boys at church who were my friends. There was Newt, who lived with us and helped Dad on the farm. And there was Larry, my Sunday school teacher, who I adored. Most of all there was Dad. Even though he was demanding and sometimes mean, I knew he cared about me and would keep me safe. He took me from Cedars and gave me a home and a new life. I knew he would protect me from my old life as best he could. He wasn't a perfect dad, but he was a decent person who was there for me. Mostly he helped me see I would never have to settle for men like George in my life.

We got upstairs, where Mom had set coffee and cookies on the table. Everyone got a cookie and a cup of coffee. When we all finished, Dad said, "Well, we need to go to church soon." Thankfully Marvin took the hint and told Josephine they needed to leave. She hugged me too long as she left, but I wanted her to go. And after she left, I missed her.

I was glad Melody was there. We had a little time before church. Even though we didn't talk much, I felt she understood my sadness. And, thankfully, I don't think she told anyone about what she had seen. She stuck by me as a friend. I think she understood this was hard for me, even though she didn't fully understand the situation.

Mom and Dad cared, but this situation also frustrated them. We never talked about it, but I heard them talking to each other about calling the social worker and "fixing this thing." I knew the folks wanted me to forget it and move on. They didn't realize this was impossible to do. I wasn't able to work out this grief with anyone, and so I pushed it down. Even though the sadness was there, I also found strength from Mom and Dad and the church. They taught me to pray, read my Bible and move on from this unfortunate situation. But the sadness and fear remained.

Sadly, this would not be the last time Josephine came out to the farm unannounced. But the next time Dad had a plan so I wouldn't have to see them at all.

Chapter 8

Hiding

"What's for lunch?" I asked, getting in the car. Newt didn't answer, so I asked again, "Did you make something, or are we going out to the café?"

Mom and Dad had left for the weekend. Mom usually had a delicious Sunday dinner waiting when we got home from church. Or sometimes we would go to Seward to Johnson's restaurant. They always had a Sunday buffet, with the best-fried chicken in the county. But I didn't know what kind of lunch we'd get that day.

Again, Newt said nothing for a while. Then he finally spoke, "We're going over to Cindy's folk's place for the afternoon."

Now I was worried. "Why are we going over there?"

"Something happened at the farm, and we can't go back there."

Now the car was silent. Newt's words caused various scenarios to pass through my mind. Was there a fire? Had someone robbed the place? Were Mom and Dad hurt and

Newt just wasn't telling me? Terrifying thoughts filled my mind, but I said nothing.

Mom and Dad were in Hesston for the weekend. Having them gone put me on edge, but they had left me in good hands. Newt was another safe male in my new life. As an older teen, Newt had come to live with Mom and Dad as a hired man. But he'd always been more than a hired man; he was a part of the family. He'd married Cindy, and they now lived on their own.

We continued to drive to an unfamiliar part of Milford. I did not know where we were going. I trusted Newt, and I knew he wouldn't take me anywhere unsafe. But it still scared me to be going to a strange place with people I didn't know. This had happened many times with Josephine. When I didn't know where I was going or who would be there, it always made me feel unsafe.

My anxiety continued to rise as Newt drove in silence. I could tell he was tense about something, but he also seemed mad. His hands gripped the steering wheel so tightly that his knuckles were white. If the house had burned down or if something had happened to Mom and Dad, he wouldn't be mad like this. Something or someone else must be the source of his irritation.

We pulled into a driveway and drove up to a house. It was a place I'd never seen before. The house was older, one story and mustard yellow with a small porch. The yard had a detached garage. I guessed this was Cindy's parents' house. Anxiety rose in me from a hidden, nameless place. It triggered a secret nonverbal anxiety in me that came from all the times I had been with Josephine and Frank, going to visit strangers. This emotional, nonverbal memory was potent. It overtook my body even though I couldn't have told anyone about it. I walked into the house with my senses on high alert.

My stress lessened a little when I saw Cindy. Her bright smile, dancing eyes, and the long blond hair were a welcome sight. She walked over and said, "This is my Mom and Dad," pointing to two people standing beside her. "We're going to stay here awhile. I'm sure Newt told you…"

Bewildered, I didn't speak, but the look on my face must have answered her question. She turned to Newt and said, "You told her what was going on."

His silence was the answer.

I could hear the frustration as she said, "Newt, tell her what's going on."

Now my eyes were on Newt. My mouth was quiet, but I was screaming inside my head, *Yes, what is going on?*

"Kathy, your mom and some of those other people are at the farm again. They came just as I finished choring. I drove past the place later and they were still there sitting in their car. Floyd told me if they pulled a stunt like this again, I shouldn't let them see you."

"We'll spend the afternoon with my folks," said Cindy. "Our apartment is too small for us all to stay the whole afternoon. We didn't know where else to go, so we came here."

I had a lot of questions going through my mind, but the only thing that came out was, "When are Mom and Dad coming home?"

Newt said he didn't know for sure but thought sometime late that afternoon or early evening.

We all ate lunch and then I followed Newt downstairs to a living/TV room with two padded swivel chairs, both a mix of olive green, orange, and mustard yellow. Between the two chairs was an olive-green couch and on the opposite wall were bookshelves with a TV sitting in the middle.

I watched sports on TV most of the afternoon. It was boring. There was nothing to do, but we had to stay there to avoid my biological family back at the farm. I was the one with the stupid mom who only lived 30 minutes away. It was my dumb mom who wouldn't follow the rules.

As I sat alone in the basement, my lips and chin trembled. Holding my breath, I tried to stop the tears from coming. No one, I thought, could understand the fear and shame I felt. Here was my past invading my present, the same as it had a few weeks earlier, when Josephine and the others came out to the farm unexpectedly. That had been scary, too. And now they were out there again. Would they keep doing this and one day come out and take me with them? If they kidnapped me, would Mom and Dad care? Did they love me? Did they care about me enough to keep me? Maybe they would be glad I was gone.

Breathing in slowly, I felt like I couldn't get enough air. The headache that was always there grew even stronger. Swallowing hard, I tried to hold back the tears.

"Do you need anything, Kathy?" Cindy's voice broke into my thoughts. She was halfway down the stairs. Before turning to look at her, I opened my eyes wide, then blinked. I didn't want her to see I was about to cry.

"I'm okay," I said with a smile on my face as I twisted toward her.

"I think we'll be going soon," she said, her voice comforting.

Maybe she could tell how distressed I felt even though I'd tried to hide it as best I could. I leaned back on the couch and pulled my legs close to my body. There was a crocheted afghan blanket on the couch, and I pulled it over my body. I heard the lively conversation and laughter from Cindy and her parents upstairs. Then my thoughts drifted back to my old life. Josephine seemed to love me. But she had allowed the welfare people to take me. In my young mind, that meant she didn't care about me enough to keep me. She didn't love me enough to stay away from the alcohol, the bars, and the men.

Now things were out of my control. I couldn't do anything about the crap Josephine was pulling. Maybe Mom and Dad would get too fed up with the hassle and send me away, send me back to Cedars. My greatest fear was that they would send me back. If they did that, I would lose another family. I would lose my new little nieces and nephews I had grown to love so much. With this thought, my chest tightened, and tears welled in my eyes. I quickly wiped them away.

But the dark thoughts kept coming. If Mom and Dad sent me back to Cedars, I would lose all my new friends at church, the children and the adults. Maybe these people would miss me a little, perhaps even be sad, but none of them would come and get me. If Floyd and Erma, who had taken in other foster children, couldn't deal with the problems of my life, none of them would try. I had always known no one in this new family, church, or community needed me to make them complete. They were already whole; I was the broken piece that needed them.

These thoughts filled my mind as I sat in the basement. Finally, Newt called down, "Come on, we're going home."

"Are they still there?" I asked when I got to the top of the stairs.

"I hope not; it's been long enough. Anyway, I've got to get home to do the evening chores before it gets dark."

We put on our coats and piled back into Newt's car. Cindy sat in front this time.

As we drove away from Cindy's parents and started toward home, I again got nervous. What would we find at home? My stomach tightened, and my chest felt heavy as we got closer. When we got within view of our house, I glued my face to the car window. But as the front of the house came into view, I saw no cars there. The tightness in my chest lessened a little. Newt must have felt it was safe, too, because he pulled into the long lane that led to the house. We got to the house and continued to the back driveway that led to the garage. They weren't on this side of the house either. *Good,* I thought, *they're gone.*

We all got out of the car. Newt headed to the grain silo to hook up the tractor to the feeder and fill it with grain to start the evening chores.

Back in the house, Cindy settled in the family room and turned on the TV. I went back to my room, turned on the radio, and lay on the bed. Helen Reddy's song "I am Woman" was playing. As I listened to her robust voice and the powerful message of this song, I moved my legs up in the air and held them there as my hands supported my butt. Putting my legs up and swinging them back and forth released some of the tension in my body. For the first time that day, I relaxed. I could only truly relax when I was by myself. Music also helped, and some songs made me feel empowered and energized. It felt safe being alone because I didn't have to worry about anyone else's emotions, only my own.

Soon voices came from the kitchen. I opened my door and realized Mom and Dad were home. I ran out of my room and gave them each a hug. As we were talking, Newt came in from choring. Dad immediately went out to the washroom and talked to Newt. They weren't talking loudly, but I knew what they were saying. Newt was telling him what happened, and Dad was getting angry.

When they finished talking, we all sat down to eat. There was tension in the air, and it was all my fault. After supper, Newt and Cindy went home, and Mom and I cleaned up the dishes. I went into the living room and sat with Dad to watch TV. As I walked past his chair to sit on the couch, he didn't look at me or acknowledge my presence. Usually, when I came into the room, he would make a joking comment or at least ask me to get him something, such as a glass of tea. But this time he sat there with his hands clenched in a fist, his mouth shut tight, and he wouldn't even look at me. I'm sure he was mad at Josephine, but I was the reason she had come, so I felt he was also mad at me. My presence had brought this mess into his life, and now he had to figure out how to stop it.

After a while, I went back to my room and got my clothes and books ready for the next day. Tomorrow, Monday, would start a new week. I wished it could be a fresh start for me, but I knew it would not. The fear of Mom and Dad sending me back to Cedars filled me, and so did the terror of Josephine possibly coming to take me herself. Dad's anger and frustration about the situation also scared me. I didn't really think he blamed me, but I felt it was my fault. And whether or not he meant to, when Dad was angry, other people suffered, and I would suffer for this mess.

I brushed my teeth, told Mom and Dad good night and went to bed. As I lay there in the stillness, I said my usual prayers. Along with many others, I prayed for Pat and Josephine. As I thought about them in this loving way, my chest again tightened. Tears came hard and fast and I rolled over before my ears got flooded. I buried my head in the pillow to silence the loud sobs. I didn't want Mom and Dad to hear me. They wouldn't understand, and it might make them even angrier to know I missed Josephine and Pat.

She had been here today, and I hadn't seen her. Maybe she'd brought Pat along. For much of the day she had sat there in the car and waited for me, but I never came. I, too, had waited for her at Cedars for nearly five months, and she had never come for me. These thoughts brought the loud sobs again, and I buried my head deeper into the pillow. She must have been so sad sitting here all day waiting. Maybe she thought I didn't love her anymore, didn't care about her, didn't want to see her. But that wasn't true. She was my mom, and I loved her and wanted to see her. But I also didn't want to see her. I didn't want to go back to her life, yet a part of me still wanted her in my life. If I stayed here, living with my new family, I knew Josephine could not be a part of my life. It would be too messy. Also,

Mom and Dad knew, as I did, it would not be safe for me.

Mom and Dad went to Lincoln a few days later and talked to my social worker. To ensure my safety, they decided that Josephine must now have supervised visits. We did these at the social worker's office in Lincoln. These visits were awkward. We didn't have much in common anymore, so there wasn't a lot to talk about. Finally, the visits ended altogether.

The canyon between Josephine and me continued to widen. This brought a little peace and calm to my life, but the pain it caused was never far from the surface. How could I cut out part of myself that had been there my whole life? How can a 12-year-old child let go of one family to have another family? It would have been easier to cut out my heart.

Chapter 9

Cousins

Sunshine warmed my face through the car window as we drove out of Seward, passing familiar sights. My stomach was full from the delicious fried chicken dinner at Johnson's Restaurant. Sitting in the back seat, I looked at the two heads in the front. I was trusting Mom and Dad more, and the bond between us was getting stronger. The agony of leaving my biological family was lessening so that I could focus on moving on with my new family.

We drove along, and I didn't ask where we were going. Usually we headed straight home on Sundays after dinner for a rather dull afternoon, so I didn't pay much attention to the direction of the car until I realized Dad drove past the usual gravel road that led to our farm. Even then, I didn't think much about it. He would often drive around the country roads looking at the crops and the fields he farmed.

As we drove, I started to space out. This was even more boring than being at home on Sunday afternoon. But Dad kept driving for so long that I couldn't help wonder what was happening. Dad liked to watch football and sleep in his recliner on Sunday afternoons.

I finally got up the nerve to ask, "Where are we going? When are we going home?"

We're visiting someone," Dad answered.

"Who are we going to visit?"

"Just wait. You'll see.

But I couldn't wait, so I kept asking, "Are we going to visit Melody's family?" Melody was one of my best friends at church, and I would love to spend the afternoon with her.

"No," Mom said.

So I kept naming other families from church. Even though Mom and Dad knew many people in the area and had lots of family, I only focused on church people. That's usually who we visited if we went out on Sundays.

We drove all around the countryside that afternoon. I kept asking Mom and Dad where we were going, but they wouldn't tell me. I was anxious and excited. It was easy for me to get confused on the country roads, and for most of the time, I didn't know where we were. Finally, the questioning became a game as I kept saying names of people I thought we might visit and Dad and Mom would reply, no, not them. Finally, we came to a place that looked familiar. This was a yard I knew well.

"Oh, Sandy and Sheila's home," I said, bouncing my head from the back seat to the front. I jumped out of the car as soon as it stopped and ran to the door.

Sandy, Sheila, and Joyce were all waiting. They must have known we were coming.

These were my new cousins, and I loved being with them. Sandy was a year older, and Sheila was a year younger than me. There were three boys in the family besides the girls. Two of the boys, Tom and Don, were older, and John was younger. This was the family of Mom's younger brother, Joe. But tragedy had struck this family when Joe died two years ago during heart surgery. He was only 40.

I remember being at their house after the funeral. Mom told Sandy and Sheila that I would understand what they were going through because I had just lost my father, meaning Frank.

But this shared loss was probably another reason I liked Sandy and Sheila. We always had fun talking, playing games or exploring their farm. So that afternoon we spent the whole time there. Mom and Dad visited with Joyce, and we girls went off together. We ate supper there and then went home. What a fun time!

***

Sandy and Sheila were not the only new family I gained. Mom and Dad both had large families, but I got to know more people on Mom's side of the family. I developed a close relationship with Mom's sister Nola and her husband, Archie, during my high school years.

Mom's dad, Grandpa Yeackley, was another person I got to know well. He was an interesting man, a farmer who had retired and moved into town. But he still tended an enormous vegetable garden and beautiful flowers in his front yard. Mom and I cleaned for him, and so I got to know him better during those times.

Looking back, I don't know if any of these family members ever considered me family. I think in their eyes

I always remained the girl Floyd and Erma took in. But from my perspective, they were my new family. I still had biological family, aunts and cousins, but I saw none of them anymore. And I didn't think I would see any of them again.

However, one night, a few years later, my two worlds again crashed together.

Friday night sports brought out the crowds in Milford, and the school was packed with fans, parents, and students. It was a cold winter night, but inside the gymnasium, the heat, crowd, and the noise that went along with high school basketball were uncomfortable for me. Large groups of people always made me feel uneasy. However, the excitement of being with my friends and watching the boys from my school play basketball was fun. The competition brought a sense of belonging and this was important for me. Not only was I a student at Milford High School, I had also joined the pep club. I sat with my classmates, cheering our team on to victory. There was excitement in each basket our team made, each point gained was a victory for all of us. And if the Milford Eagles won the game, then we were all winners, together.

Our team was playing well when the whistle blew for halftime. Now the gym was full of noise and people moving around. I stood up and stretched. Stepping out into the crowd in this hot, noisy gym sounded unpleasant, but I was thirsty. I walked down the creaky metal bleachers. At the bottom, I joined the flow of fans making their way to the cafeteria, where the concession stand was set up.

Halfway there someone tapped me on the shoulder. I turned and looked at the person. It was another student.

She had a Milford letter jacket on, so I knew she was on my side. Her face was familiar, but I didn't know her name.

"Are you Kathy Shorny?" she asked.

"Yes," I said.

"Your cousin is looking for you."

When she said "your cousin" I immediately thought it must be Sandy or Sheila. I thought it was strange they had asked someone else to come and get me, but I was thrilled they called me their cousin. This increased my sense of belonging.

"Where is she?" I asked.

"I'll show you," the girl said.

I followed her through the hot, noisy hallway to the other side of the gym, where the opposing team sat. Why would Sandy or Sheila be sitting on the other team's side?

We walked through the entrance that fans of visiting teams used. Now I was in enemy territory. It felt strange, but I was curious. I hadn't even considered that I might have a connection to the other team. We were playing Brainerd High that night. This was a small town I had gone to many times as a child. Aunt Betty, Josephine's sister, owned a bar there, and we often visited her. But in an attempt to forget my old life, I had made no personal connection to Brainerd that night.

Finally, we were at our destination. "Here's your cousin," the girl said and walked away. Confused, I looked at the woman and two young boys standing before me. Who were these people? I thought. And where were Sandy and Sheila?

Then the woman spoke, "Hi, Kathy. How are you doing?"

I looked at her, still bewildered by who she was and what she was doing here.

"It's me, Tanny, and you remember Ricky and Randy."

Then I realized what was going on. Tanny was Aunt Betty's daughter. Seeing her here suddenly brought my new world and my old world together. It was a little like fire and ice colliding. It shocked me that she was here. I barely said anything to her. Then my body tensed as another thought filled my mind. Who did she bring with her? Was Pat or Josephine here? Did they know about my school and the basketball games? It would be easy for them to get to me in such a vast crowd. And what if they brought Marvin and George, the ones who came out to the farm? Suddenly I didn't feel safe.

Another fear swept over me then: what if my friends and other kids at school found out my biological relatives were here? How would I explain it to them? I feared it would only set me apart even more. If people saw me with my old family, they would know I didn't really belong.

In my fear and confusion, I barely talked to Tanny. She seemed happy to see me and asked how I was doing. But I had difficulty answering her. This situation was confusing, disorienting and scary for me, but it was also sad. I loved Tanny. She had been a safe person in my childhood. She was someone I felt really cared about me. She didn't get drunk like Josephine, so I felt safe with her. She was someone I had cared for so much as a child I named my favorite doll after her. This evening I had the chance to get reacquainted with her. But because of my fear of not fitting in and of being exposed as a fake, I barely said anything to her. She probably thought I didn't care.

But my new life was becoming more of my identity than any part of my old life. The episode with Tanny proved that. I was being shaped by my new family and community. No longer did I see myself as a poor foster child from an abusive, alcoholic family. More and more, I was forgetting about my old world and growing into my new one.

Chapter 10

Community

"Cheryl, come over here right now," I heard Mrs. Moser call to my new friend. "What's going on here? Why is Kathy standing against the wall crying? You were playing nicely a few minutes ago. What happened?"

"I didn't do anything, Mrs. Moser. We're just playing hide and seek."

This happened on the freezing cold playground right before Christmas break. Many of the students had complained as we walked out of the school building. We all wanted to stay inside and play games in the classroom. But as children we had no choice.

When we got to the playground, Cheryl, one of my new friends, asked me to play hide and seek.

I said, "Sure," and the game began.

"Come and hide over here with me. I know a good spot where she'll never find us," Cheryl said as one of the other girls started to count. We hid together, and it took a long time for someone to find us.

Cheryl explained to Mrs. Moser that the other girls had taken their turns being "it," and I was the last one.

"Kathy, come over here." Mrs. Moser motioned with her arm for me to come to her. "What's going on here? Were you playing hide and seek with these girls?"

"Yes, we were having fun playing. Cheryl even let me hide with her. She's been nice." I was trying to protect Cheryl because I knew if they saw me as a tattletale the other children might not want to play with me.

"Then why were you standing against the wall with your hands over your eyes, shaking and crying?"

"I wasn't crying, Mrs. Moser. I was 'it,' and it was my turn to count. I had my hands over my eyes so I wouldn't see where the other girls had hidden. That's how you play Hide and Go Seek."

"I know how you play Hide and Go Seek, child. I've been a teacher for more years than you've been alive. But why were you crying? I saw your body shaking as you were standing against the wall."

Having only been at the school three weeks, I wasn't sure how to act. I still hadn't figured out Mrs. Moser, my fifth-grade teacher. She got angry with other children, and I didn't want to upset her. I didn't want to risk her getting angry at me if I continued to defend myself, so I stayed quiet.

Then Cheryl said, "Mrs. Moser, it's freezing out here. We're all shaking and shivering from the cold. Kathy was probably just shaking from the cold."

"Is that correct, Kathy?"

Not wanting to say the wrong thing, I nodded. But my heart felt happy. I realized I had a friend who spoke up for me. She risked getting into trouble with Mrs. Moser to say what I couldn't.

Cheryl was one of the first children I met when I came to live in Milford. She had come to my house a few times. Her family had a dairy farm close to our farm. Mom and Dad were trying to help me get to know other children, so they invited Cheryl over. But being friends outside of school and being friends in school were often different. A child risks losing school friends if they include the new kid in their group. But Cheryl didn't seem to fear the rejection of the other children when she asked me to play hide and seek that day. Now it appeared she didn't fear the wrath of Mrs. Moser either.

"Okay, thank you, Cheryl. Thanks for playing with Kathy and helping her feel welcome at school. Keep up the good work."

We all ran away from where Mrs. Moser was standing to another part of the playground. The other girls didn't ignore me as we huddled together to stay warm and whisper about how mean Mrs. Moser could be. It wasn't long before we heard the loud, sharp sound of her whistle, that meant it was time to go inside.

The last day of school before the Christmas break was a good one for me. It was so different from what I had experienced only a year before. When I lived in Lincoln with my biological family, others rarely protected me. I still felt like the kid that nobody wanted to be around. But today in my new life, two important people had shown that they were looking out for me and wanted what was best for me. This helped me see myself in a new way.

Teachers were always a significant part of my life. When

I lived with Josephine, they served as models of what it meant to be a female. Most of the women I encountered in my home life were poor, many of them addicted to alcohol, sex, or both. But my teachers were different. They dressed nicely and cared about their appearance—not to attract men but to look smart and professional. Their example told me that women were more than objects to be used by men. They represented another way to be a female, and I wanted to follow their example.

The only teachers I remember taking a particular interest in me were my fourth- and fifth-grade teachers. Mrs. Johnson was my fourth-grade teacher at St. Mary's in Lincoln. She saw I was a bright little girl living in challenging circumstances. She didn't just see the poverty, she saw *me*.

Mrs. Moser also saw me in a positive way. Even if I did something wrong, I thought she would give me the benefit of the doubt. She must have known I came from a difficult life in Lincoln. I believe this softened her toward me. Mrs. Moser won my heart that day. In protecting me from what she thought was the cruelty of other children, I realized she was an adult I could trust, and after that I always tried to please her.

I even wrote a poem about Mrs. Moser and what an excellent teacher she was for me. I wrote the poem in school, and it stayed in my desk. I never meant to show it to anyone, but the last two weeks of that school year I contracted the measles, which meant I never made it back to my fifth-grade class. Mrs. Moser cleaned out my desk for me and left my things with the school secretary for my folks to pick up. When Mom brought my things home, I looked through this stuff for the poem. It was not there.

Although I was a little embarrassed that Mrs. Moser had read my poem, I was also glad. I could have never told her the things I put in the poem, but this way she still knew how I felt about her.

Dad and Mom were the ones who brought me into this community and new life. But like Mrs. Moser, many other people helped me feel a sense of belonging. Church and community people also helped Mom and Dad when the challenges of caring for foster children and caring for biological children collided.

Loree, Mom and Dad's youngest biological child, had been born with a physical disability which created many challenges in her life. When I came to live with the folks, Loree was a young adult in her early 20s, just starting out in life. Because of her disability, Loree wasn't steady on her feet. The icy winters of the midwest were challenging for her, so she moved to warm, sunny Phoenix.

It was difficult for Mom and Dad to have Loree so far away, so they became snowbirds. This meant they went to Phoenix for part of the winter. Many people did this to get away from the cold winters. But Mom and Dad's primary drive was to help Loree. But that created a new problem of how to care for the foster kids while they were in Phoenix. Mom and Dad came up with a creative solution.

Rather than farming me and Mark, another foster child who lived with us during most of my time with the folks, out to other families in the community, they invited trusted adults to come to our house and live with us. Mom and Dad's leaving uprooted our lives, but staying in our familiar home still felt safer than leaving.

It was challenging to have Mom and Dad gone, but

also relaxing in a way. I no longer felt the pressure of trying to please Dad and the fear of getting it wrong. Plus, we got to know other people from the community and the church. These were good experiences because I felt safe with all the people who stayed with us, like Gary and Rosemary.

Gary and Rosemary were not from our church, but like many people in the community, they were relatives of Mom or Dad. Rosemary was a quiet, kind woman. Her husband, Gary, was a fun-loving jokester, much like Dad.

One night at home, Rosemary and I had cooked supper, and we all sat down to eat. We were sharing stories from our day when we heard the dog bark. The dog was a beautiful, sable-colored male collie named Laddie. Dad always got collies. They were smart herding dogs with an easy temperament. He trained them well, and they helped herd the cattle.

A little barking from Laddie was not unusual. Maybe he saw a squirrel or was warning another animal to stay out of his territory. But prolonged barking meant something was not right.

"What's wrong with that dog?" Rosemary asked as she looked across the living room to the patio doors where Laddie stood barking.

"I don't know if I've ever heard him bark this much," I said, looking in the same direction. The pleasant supper conversation stopped as the barking got louder and more intense. My body stiffened as fear-infused questions entered my mind. Was someone out there? Would someone break into the house and hurt us? Were Josephine and some of her men out there? I then realized how safe Laddie always made me feel. I knew he was trying to protect me now, but protect me from what?

Gary pushed his chair back and walked over to the patio door.

"It looks like he's got something up in the tree." Gary spoke up loudly so we could hear him over the barking.

If Laddie had something, it was probably an animal rather than a person. So, with more curiosity than fear, I went with Mark and Rosemary to join Gary.

"What is it?" Rosemary asked.

"I don't know. Let me get my shoes on and my flashlight out of the truck."

Gary walked to the mudroom and put on his shoes and coat.

Mark, Rosemary, and I continued to look out the patio door and up into the tree as Laddie continued to bark. Laddie had chased something up in the tree, and he wouldn't stop barking and let it come down unless someone gave him a command.

"I'm gonna see if I can help," Mark said. He put on his shoes and jacket and went out in the dark, cold, February night.

Soon we saw Gary's flashlight bobbing on the ground as he came around the side of the house. Mark walked behind him.

As Gary shone the beam up into the tree, we saw what all the excitement was about. Several branches high sat a large, gray raccoon snarling down at Laddie.

"Down Laddie," Gary said as he held the raccoon in place with the flashlight beam. Laddie sat quietly by Gary, but his ears stayed alert, and he never took his eyes off the raccoon. He was ready to jump into action if the raccoon made a move.

Gary turned to Mark and said, "Get the rifle out of the garage and a couple of bullets."

Mark walked back into the garage and returned with the rifle and bullets. He handed them to Gary as Gary passed the flashlight to him. As the beam of the light moved away from the raccoon, Laddie barked again as if sensing the animal was about to escape.

"Shine the light up in the tree, on the coon," Gary said to Mark. Then he unlocked the handle of the gun from the barrel and slid the bullets in.

As I saw Gary putting the bullets in, I knew what was coming next. I didn't want to see that, so I walked down the hall to my bedroom. A shiver went through my body when I heard the two gunshots.

When I walked back into the kitchen, Rosemary was already sitting at the table finishing her supper. I sat back in my place and ate too.

"Wow, that was some shot," I heard Mark's voice as he and Gary walked back into the house.

"Well, it wasn't too hard to shoot it down with Laddie's barking keeping it up there and you shining the flashlight on it," Gary said.

"So, you got it," Rosemary said as the two males sat back down at the table.

"Yeah, it's a nice big one, too. I should be able to get $15 or 20 dollars for the skin. I'll take it over to that guy in Beaver Crossing tomorrow."

"What are you going to do with the money?" Mark asked.

"Well, it's not my money. I used your dad's gun and bullets, and you helped me by shining the light on it." Gary paused a moment and then said, "I know. Why don't we use the money to all go out for supper this weekend?"

"Sure, that sound's good," Mark and I said together.

"Where should we go?" Rosemary asked.

"How about Valentino's," I said. I wanted to go there because it was the best pizza place around. Our youth group often went there, and I would sometimes go with friends.

"That would be good. There's shopping I need to do in Lincoln, and we could go eat and then go shopping."

The next Friday night, the last week Gary and Rosemary stayed with us, we all went to Valentino's and ate pizza with the money Gary got from the raccoon skin. I missed them when they left. They were a fun couple and there was less tension in the house when they were there. But it was also good to have Mom and Dad back.

Mom and Dad gave me safety and stability and met my physical needs for food, shelter, and clothing. We also had fun times together, but a lot of those fun times happened with people from the community, like Gary and Rosemary. Church people were also significant in meeting needs for fun and connecting with others. I achieved my spiritual needs through the church, and these spiritual aspects gave me a different view of myself. I could see new worth in myself because people at church viewed me as valuable. One of these people was my junior high Sunday school teacher, Larry.

Chapter 11

Church

It was Sunday, my favorite day of the week. I was also thrilled that Larry was teaching our Sunday school class that day. He often had fun, exciting activities for us to do. However, the activity he asked us to do that day made me squirm. We were to think of a color that described our family and draw a picture.

Oh no, I thought. What family am I going to describe, my biological family or my new foster family? For the typical Bellwood Mennonite kid this was a no brainer. But it threw me into a panic. What seemed like a creative, open-ended activity became a no-win choice. If I used my new foster family, the other kids might say they weren't my real family. (Lots of people talked about "real" families when they meant biological families.) And if I spoke of my biological family, it would be clear I didn't belong here.

It was scary drawing either picture. I pulled a white piece of paper from the center of the table, picked up the red crayon and began.

Larry, who grew up at Bellwood, was a tall, lean young man with reddish-blonde hair and a light complexion. Having finished college and a voluntary service term in South America, he was now back in Milford. He was a good teacher whom I respected and had a big crush on.

After we finished drawing our pictures, it was time to share what we had done. First Sonia answered, then Michelle and Doug. They talked about life on the farm with the colors green and yellow for John Deere equipment. Another had the colors red and white for the Cornhuskers football team. With each answer, my turn came closer, and my stomach tightened. Now it was Charnelle's turn, and I heard nothing she said because my turn was next.

When Charnelle stopped talking, everyone was looking at me.

"Kathy, do you want to share your picture?" Larry asked. I knew by his kind tone that this wasn't a demand but a genuine question.

Trembling inside, I held up my picture of a bright red kitchen table. "This is the kitchen table where I lived with my biological family. I drew a red table because it represents the love and anger and fighting. All three were part of our family."

I'd put it out there. I'd talked about my biological family, showing the good and the bad. A silence fell on the group. My peers, along with Larry, appeared to think about what I said.

Finally, someone said, "My family gets angry, too."

Larry responded, "Most families have anger and love. Thanks for sharing that, Kathy." The smile on his face showed me what I shared was okay.

As I let out my breath and I leaned back in the chair, my shoulders and stomach relaxed. The last two kids shared their pictures. I sat and listened because now the focus was on them. No one stared at me or whispered that my picture was stupid. My sharing was just one of the stories that morning. I was neither special or weird. I was just part of the group. That meant everything to me!

Larry had a significant impact on my life during these transitional years. I was transitioning from my old life to a new one, and from a girl to a woman. So, besides the schoolgirl crush I had on Larry, he was also a person I respected and admired.

Larry was around the same age as Pat and his friends. But those males were horrible, and Larry was terrific. Those sexually perverted men had little education and low morals. They only saw themselves and what they wanted. They saw girls and women as sexual objects, even those who were only 10 years old.

Now I was 12, and Larry was in my life. He was absolutely everything those young men were not. His classes and the way he treated me helped me see myself differently. Instead of seeing myself as a sexual object to be used by men, now I saw my power coming through knowledge and education.

With the example of people at Bellwood I could strive for something more than self-gain. By helping others, I filled an emptiness in me. Most important, I did not need to belong to a man to have safety in my life. (Not that there wasn't the expectation I would marry a man; this was still a fairly patriarchal church community.)

Many people at Bellwood, including Larry, helped me see the value of having a relationship with God. Their relationship with God gave them meaning and purpose and this was who I wanted to become. This view of myself was not fully formed, but it was starting.

The people at Bellwood were not the only ones who saw me as a valuable person and encouraged my relationship with God. There were other people in the larger faith community that helped shape this identity. Most church events took place at Bellwood. But once a year there were revivals either at the high school or at Riverside, a campground just outside Milford. These events also helped shape my new identity.

One prominent Mennonite evangelist, Myron Augsburger, came to Milford for several years and did revivals at Riverside. Because my mom enjoyed hosting, Pastor Augburger and his team came to supper one night at our house.

***

Usually in the summer we ate supper later in the evening, around 6:30, but tonight we were eating at five. Important guests were coming, and they would need to leave early.

As I stood in the bathroom, waiting for my curling iron to heat, I heard the doorbell ring. The guests had arrived. I knew Mom wanted me in the kitchen to help get the meal on. Thankfully, we had already set the table with the white tablecloth and the good china.

When the red light flashed, I quickly wrapped my short, brown hair around the burning hot metal barrel and studied my reflection. My hair wasn't perfect, but it would do. The guests were here, and Mom was waiting for me. Hearing the lard sizzling in the frying pan and the delicious smell of Mom's fried chicken raised my level of anxiety. Oh, no, if Mom's frying the chicken already, that meant the meal would soon be ready.

As I walked out of the bathroom into the hall, I heard the shower running in Dad's bathroom at the other end of the house. Good, I thought, Dad is in from choring. But now there was even more pressure to get the meal on the table.

Entering the living room, I hoped to walk through to the kitchen without being seen. But not wanting to be rude, I stopped and looked at the men sitting on the olive-green couch along the far wall of the room. They were all dressed in dark suits. This was typical for pastors ready for a worship service. The sweet smell of their cologne filled the air. I hoped they wouldn't look back at me. If they didn't look back and just ignored me, as often happened with adult company, then I could quietly slip into the kitchen. But to my surprise, the three looked up at me. *Oh no,* I thought, *now I have to stop and say something.*

The next thing that happened was unexpected: the three men all stood up at the same time. The first one held out his hand and said, "Good evening." Instinctively I went over to him, shook his hand and said hello. Then the other two men held out their hands and we exchanged the same greeting. Hearing our voices, Mom stepped into the living room.

"This is our girl, Kathy. Kathy, this is Reverend Augsburger." Mom introduced the other two men, but I don't remember their names. I said hi again, feeling awkward because they were standing, and I really didn't know what else to say or do. Finally, they sat down, and Mom told me to help her in the kitchen. As we turned, Dad was coming into the living room, fresh from his shower and dressed for the evening church service. *Oh good,* I thought, *now Dad can talk to the guests, and Mom and I can focus on the meal.*

Soon we were all sitting around the dining table. "Reverend Augsburger, would you say the prayer?" Dad asked.

He said yes, and we all bowed our heads. For the next 20 minutes, we enjoyed delicious fried chicken and mashed potatoes with gravy. Mom had also pulled out the extra sweet corn we had shucked, cooked, and frozen only a month earlier. Large, juicy, red beefsteak tomatoes from the garden provided the salad part of the meal. Only the bread had been bought at the store because Mom hadn't had time that day to make the pull-apart bread she usually made for company.

The three men declined dessert because they needed to get to Riverside for the evening service.

After Myron Augsburger and the two other men left, Mom and I cleaned up the meal. Then we all went to the church service.

That night had a powerful impact on my life and my faith. These men all stood up when I entered the room. This had never happened before; it made me feel valued and respected. Because they stood up and greeted me when I came into the room, I felt like they saw me as a fellow human being and not just a pre-teen kid or worse, a foster child that didn't really belong. This respectful treatment also gave me great respect and admiration for the three men, especially Pastor Augsburger.

Because I felt so valued and respected by Pastor Augsburger, I could connect with the sermons he gave each night. He led revivals for several years in Milford, and I always looked forward to them.

Many of the lessons I learned from Pastor Augsburger's sermons continue to guide my life today. One of those sermons was about Og, who slept on an iron bed. In his sermon, Pastor Augsburger said this is the only time the Bible mentions Og. And the only thing said about him was he had an iron bed. The lesson was there were people in the Bible mentioned many times for how they served and followed God's call. Og was mentioned only once, and because of something he had, not for what he did. So how will we be remembered, by what we have or for what we do for God? This was a powerful lesson, and I can still hear Pastor Augsburger's booming voice in my head. He would list various things the priests or prophets did to serve God, then he would say, "But Og, he had an iron bed!" Then he'd say more about the prophets followed by, "But Og, he had an iron bed!"

Another lesson was about a farmer who came home from church one Sunday evening and saw people stealing watermelons out of his field. The farmer turned his car into the field and shone the headlights on the group to let them know he had caught them. He asked his wife to call the sheriff. Then he told the group to stay there because the sheriff was coming.

The farmer waited and waited, but the sheriff didn't come. Finally, after waiting for an hour with no sheriff, he told the people to come out of the field and go home. To the farmer's sad amazement, when the group came out, the sheriff was right there in the middle. The lesson of this story was that we can't claim to be one thing and act in an entirely different way.

The last story from those teachings was about a pastor who was shaking hands with people after his sermon. One man came up to him and said, "Good sermon, preacher. And you know if God ever calls me the way he did when I was 15, then I will follow him. If I ever hear God's call that strongly again, I'll come back to God."

The pastor replied, "Sir, if you ever hear a whisper of God calling you, then you need to run to him because you're not 15 years old anymore and you've grown spiritually deaf. So I recommend that if you hear God calling you at all, you run to him."

This is a message that has stayed with me all these years. I realized I didn't want to get too far away from God that I no longer heard the call. I did not and still don't want to grow spiritually deaf.

Feeling valued by pastors, Sunday school teachers, Mennonite Youth Fellowship leaders and many others in the church helped me enjoy church services of all kinds. Many of the lessons made lifelong impressions on me. There were other fun things I did with people from the church that also taught me valuable lessons.

Another part of my new identity and growing faith in God was serving. Service and mission work are integral parts of being a Mennonite, especially in the context of my home and church. My parents served on committees at Bellwood—Dad on property and Mom on any committee that needed a good cook. Mom was always involved in WMSA, which stood for Women's Missionary

Service Auxiliary. This group of women met once a month at church and carried out various mission projects. Mom and Dad also helped with other church and community activities, including the Mennonite Central Committee (MCC) meat canning and making soap for MCC at our farm. They also were involved in the MCC sales in Kansas before any were held in Nebraska. The year after I left for college, Mom was an instigating factor in starting the Et Cetera Shop, a Mennonite thrift store in Seward. And years later she served on the steering committee to get an MCC sale in Nebraska. So, you might say service was in their blood, and they passed this along to me.

Sometimes service projects were fun, sometimes they involved hard work, and occasionally the service project was just plain gross.

***

"Floyd, I need you and Newt to set up the tables in the garage. And if you could get those big plastic tubs from the shed that would be helpful, too," Mom said.

"Sure. We'll get to it as soon as Newt's done choring. What's going on today?" Dad asked as he took the last drink of coffee from his cup.

Always attentive, Mom refilled his coffee immediately. "Claridy and the girls are coming around nine, and she's bringing soap from the motel. We're washing it, and then we'll send it to MCC."

"That's a smart idea," Dad said. "It's good to reuse stuff rather than throwing it away." He was looking at me sitting at the other end of the table as he said this. This statement was a parental lesson he felt compelled to teach me: Be thrifty. Save, don't waste.

Mom knew he was talking to me. She didn't need lessons on saving or being thrifty. She was the expert. I was the young Padawan who needed to learn these lessons.

I wasn't thinking as much about being thrifty as about having fun this morning. My girlfriends from church would arrive soon. Claridy, too. She was kind, positive, and fun to be around.

This morning we were doing a GMSA activity. GMSA stood for Girls' Mission and Service Auxiliary. At the time, I didn't know this was part of a larger organization of the Mennonite church started in 1922, the Mennonite Women's Missionary Society, which today lives on in the church as Mennonite Women.

The job before us this morning was a rather disgusting one: cleaning off the soap left over in the bathrooms from the local motel. I think Mom and Claridy had come up with the idea. I don't think the larger GMSA organization promoted it. Claridy and her husband owned the motel on the interstate at the Milford exit. Because of this connection and Mom's and Claridy's creativity, they came up with the idea together.

After I washed the breakfast dishes, Mom and I carried towels to the garage. Dad and Newt had already set up the tables. There were two six-foot-long tables set up lengthways. At the end of each table was a large tub about twelve inches tall and 24 around. After Mom and I laid down the towels on the tables and filled the containers with water, we heard a car coming down the lane. Claridy and the girls were here. When the car rolled to a stop, everyone piled out. It was a hot summer day, so everyone wore shorts, T-shirts and flip-flops.

"Michelle, come and help me with the tubs," Claridy said as she opened the trunk. They each lifted out a tub and carried them to the garage.

"Okay girls, this is the soap that's left over when people stay at the motel. This is about two months' worth. We usually throw it away, but I realized that was a waste of perfectly good soap, so I saved it. This morning we will wash the soap, so it's nice and clean. Make sure you get all the little hairs off. Then you'll put it on the towels to dry."

We all stood in there staring at Claridy. I think we were all repeating the same sentence in our heads, "Get all the little hairs off." Until that point, washing soap had not seemed like such a bad job. How bad could it be to wash soap that by definition was already clean? But the thought of "little hairs" put a new spin on it. Soon Mom broke the silence.

"Let's go, girls. Just put the soap in the water, clean off the hairs or anything else that's on it and lay it on the towels to dry." As Mom said this, she showed us what to do. Madge was the first one to jump in. She took a handful of the small bars and put them in the water. I went in next. Finally, Charnelle and Michelle started. Charnelle had a gentle nature and didn't say much as she slowly put the soap in the water and rubbed it between her hands. Michelle, however, was always more verbal.

"How are we supposed to get this hair off it doesn't just slide off? Can I have a toothpick to scrape it off?'

"Just use your fingernail to get it off," Claridy suggested.

Claridy was Michelle's aunt and could speak to her more freely about what she should do. But Michelle would not give up about wanting a toothpick. Finally, Mom went into the house and brought back a handful of toothpicks and laid them on the towels. We were all thankful for Michelle's persistence. The toothpicks were helpful in getting the thick embedded hairs off. We also used them to catch the hairs floating in the water and put them in the trash. We didn't like the hairs continually touching our hands in the water.

This may have been the only time we washed soap for an activity. I suspect Mom and Claridy were just as grossed out by the hairs, especially the thick black ones, as we girls were. It was a good idea to reuse all this soap. It seemed like a waste to just throw it all away. But it was not the most enjoyable service job we did for the church.

Some things are good to do but also disgusting, like washing soap. There were also adventurous things I experienced with my new family. Some of these things were good, some were fun, but some were terrifying. However, when we do terrifying things and don't die, we can gain a greater sense of accomplishment and self-esteem.

Chapter 12

Scary but Safe

Camping at Wilson Lake with Janet and Stan's family was one of those adventurous things I did in my childhood. Being with them felt fun and relaxing, the way I imagined things would feel in a "typical" family. An exciting and sometimes terrifying activity was riding horse trails around the lake.

Camping with Stan & Janet

We'd finished breakfast, the dishes were clean, and the food was packed away. Next came time for my first horseback ride ever. Approaching the gigantic animal, the scents of leather, sweat, and hay filled my hyper-vigilant senses.

"She's a tame one, so you need not worry," said Stan. I knew he meant to reassure, but I barely heard him. My breath came short and fast. I stood frozen by the horse as Stan saddled him up. The horse towered above me as my sense of control slipped.

"Make sure you get that cinch as tight as you can, so the saddle doesn't slip when you're riding," he told Marty, their only son. "Here, let me help you." Stan pulled hard on the large cinches that held the saddles on the horses.

"Come on, Kathy, get on. It'll be fun," encouraged Jody, my sweet, friendly younger niece. I trusted her and didn't want to spoil her ride.

"Just put your foot in the stirrup, grab the saddle horn and swing your other leg over the horse," Stan said. Soon I was sitting five feet off the ground and on top of this enormous animal, my legs splayed around its body. Getting on the horse was only the first hurdle to overcome.

"Hang onto the reins but hold them loose," he said. "Pull back to stop and give a little shake to go. When we go up a hill, lean forward with the horse, and when we go down the hill, lean back." Stan spoke patiently, but I felt it annoyed him needing to give me so much support. Even though I was the oldest child here, I obviously needed the most help.

We set out for the trail, and the swaying side to side created a comforting rhythm. The clip-clop of the horse's hooves calmed my breathing, and I slowly relaxed. Maybe this wouldn't be so bad. Perhaps I would like riding horses. As I gently moved the reins to the left, the horse moved to the left. If I moved to the right, it moved right. Wow, this was not so hard. New confidence flooded through me. I was in charge of this magnificent animal instead of the other way around. Looking down, I saw little red, purplish flowers. These wildflowers caught my attention, and their beauty calmed my body.

"Okay, we've got hills to climb."

I barely heard Stan's words in my new relaxed state. But soon I realized something was different. The horse's body was no longer flat and perpendicular with my body. Now the horse was climbing the hill, and I instinctively wanted to lean back. My breath quickened, and my chest tightened. I longed for the flat trail.

"Lean in with the horse, Kathy," Stan called back.

Rubbing the coarse, hairy body, I leaned forward. This position felt safer as the horse and I seemed more connected. Now the horse was in control. Instead of a swaying side-to-side, we jerked back and forth. Staying close to the neck of the horse, I prayed for flat ground.

"Okay, now we're headed back down." Stan had topped the hill and was disappearing down the other side. "Remember to lean back in the saddle as we go down."

Reaching the top of the hill, I didn't have a glorious summit experience. My fear overshadowed the beautiful views as terror filled my body. Even the horse seemed unsure as he tried to find a safe, steady footing. I leaned back as far as I could, the horse leaned forward as we jerked down on this steep, dangerous terrain.

I had lost control of the situation, like so many times

in my childhood where I had no power. But unlike those abusive situations, I was now surrounded by supportive people. Riding a horse down a steep hill defintely felt scary, but it also helped me see that I could navigate scary situations under the right circumstances. I didn't have to shy away from all frightening experiences as I had done with my biological family. Stan and Janet cared about me and wanted me to have a good time. They focused on my needs, not their own. That's why they were trustworthy adults. With people like that, I could overcome certain things even if they were scary.

At the end of the trail, slumping in the saddle, I sighed with relief; the ride was over. With rubbery legs and shaking body, I walked back to the campsite for lunch. Now I could relax with my feet firmly on the ground.

We made many memories together at that campfire site, sitting around the smoky fire making hobo dinners and s'mores, then sleeping on the hard, dewy ground. There were moments when I feared I was doing something wrong, and I worried Janet and Stan would disapprove of me, but the circle of the camp and the love of the family held me close and safe.

***

Not only was I able to trust Janet and Stan, but they also trusted me with important things like babysitting their children, my nieces and nephew. I enjoyed playing with Jody, Cindy, and Vicki, who were younger than me. We played with Barbie dolls, dressed up, and messed around. We even gave each other nicknames—Cindy Sue Kangaroo, Vicki Jo Eskimo, and Katherine Josephine, "the prettiest queen you've ever seen."

I also liked babysitting because it provided a fun, happy, and safe place to feel older and responsible. Usually things went smoothly, but one hot August day there was a challenge I wasn't sure how to handle.

Four-year-old Cindy walked into the house, the screen door slamming behind her. "Kathy, there's something on my back." Her short, carrot-top hair dripped with moisture, and she was sweaty and dirty.

"Shhh. We need to be quiet. Vicki's sleeping," I said. Baby Vicki was taking her afternoon nap.

"Jody said you should look on my back," Cindy said, lowering her young voice to a whisper. Jody, Marty, and Cindy had been playing outside while I stayed inside with the baby. Moving to the edge of the soft, overstuffed rocking chair, Cindy walked closer and turned around. I pushed up her T-shirt and saw something small and brown.

"Let's go into the kitchen and get a better look." We walked into the kitchen, and I took a flashlight out of the drawer. I shone the light and became alarmed.

"Oh yuck."

"What is it?"

"It's a tick."

"Can you get it out?" Cindy cried.

"Sure." I tried to sound confident.

Bugs were disgusting, and ticks were the worst. No question, I had to get it off Cindy's back, but could I do that without touching it? I knew I couldn't just grab it with tweezers and yank it off. Pulling off the body without the head would be worse than not trying at all.

Cindy continued to stand in the middle of the kitchen, with her shirt hiked over her head. She seemed to have more confidence in the process than I did. Pondering the options, I remembered something about removing ticks. If you hold a hot match to the tick, the heat will make the head pull out. This seemed like a good solution, so I fetched the matches.

Lighting a match, I let it burn for a second, then blew it out. Cindy continued to stand there. She was unaware of what was about to happen. She trusted me to care for her. As I was about to touch the tick with the match, I stopped and pulled back. This is not a good idea, I thought. Cindy could get burned if I touched the hot match to her skin. I needed a Plan B.

Cindy patiently stood there while I searched for rubbing alcohol in the bathroom. My new plan was to hold the bottle of rubbing alcohol on her back and lift it up so the alcohol would drown the tick and pull it out of her skin.

"Okay, Cindy, I need you to stand up straight and then bend over when I tell you to." She dutifully obeyed. But the longer it took, the more worried she became. I was losing confidence in myself, too. But this method worked, and I dislodged the tick without harming Cindy.

I was proud of myself for finding a solution to a problem, and also stopped myself from doing something dumb like accidentally burning my dearly loved Cindy with a match. Earning adults' trust and learning to handle difficult situations on my own was instrumental in building my confidence.

In my biological family, there weren't many opportunities to play safely with other children. When I did, the threat of the unsafe adults and older brothers loomed in the background. In contrast, playing with children at Janet's house was relaxing and fun. I didn't have to worry as much about getting in trouble, or adults getting mad and fighting. I was part of a healthy family, so I could be normal, too.

Playing dress-up

Cheers!

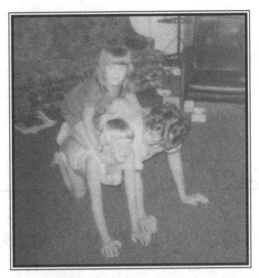

Human pyramid

Chapter 13

From Helpless to Helpful

Cooperation was crucial in my new family. Completing a task as a group built confidence and a sense of accomplishment, even though I often fought doing the work as I entered my teenage years.

"Come on, Kathy, it's time to get up," Mom said as she opened the door to my room and looked in. "Dad's already in the field getting the corn. He'll be back in about an hour, so we need to get going." When I didn't stir, she said in a stronger voice, "Come on, get up."

Today was corn day.

Slowly I pushed the covers back, sat up, and stretched. I wanted to sleep a little longer, but I knew doing so would further frustrate Mom, so I got up. I also knew this would be a fun and busy day. After I got dressed, I went out to the kitchen.

"Well, good morning sleepy head," Paulene said as she and her young daughter, Shelly, ate their breakfast. They were early birds like Mom. I was a late sleeper like Dad.

I ate my breakfast, including one of Mom's delicious cinnamon rolls, which she usually reserved for Sunday mornings and when we had company. As I put my dishes into the dishwasher, I heard Dad's old turquoise Chevy pickup. The motor thundered and stirred up dust as it raced down the lane, filled, I knew, with sweet corn.

It was a good and familiar sound, but suddenly the pressure was on. The job before us would be huge. I raced outside and saw the mountain of corn towering high in the truck bed. First we needed to make sure we had enough containers, knives (to cut off the corn tops), and a tarp to catch the husks.

When everything was ready, Shelly, Dad, and I sat on the edge of the pickup bed. I grabbed up my first ear of corn and peeled off the husk. I enjoyed the cool early morning breeze and the smell of the fresh corn, although I always feared finding a fat, juicy worm inside the husk.

At this stage, the massive pile of corn seemed overwhelming, and I found myself wishing I could still be sleeping. As a teenager, I focused on the sleep I missed rather than the satisfying work. Still, I understood that I performed an important part of this job, along with everyone else.

My immediate attention was on the ear of corn in my hand. It was important to pull back the husk carefully so I wasn't surprised by a worm. Sometimes only remnants of the worm were there—the slimy mess left behind after the top of the ear was devoured. I carefully pulled back the husks and tossed them in the pickup bed, taking care to remove as many of the silk hairs from the ear as possible. The inevitable imperfection of my efforts always evoked scolding from Mom or Dad.

If the end of the cob was long enough, I could snap it off. But if it was too short, we needed to use the large butcher knife to cut it off. This was usually a problem for me. I hacked into the cob and corn juice sprayed by my clothes, face, and glasses. After a couple of unsuccessful whacks, I usually passed the ear on to a stronger grownup.

Husking corn

Finally, the back of the pickup was empty, and we moved on to the second task. The husked and cleaned corn would then go into a large black outdoor kettle, situated safely away from the yard and house, with a fire under it to cook. The kettle was Dad's domain, to make sure we all stayed safe and didn't catch fire.

While Dad boiled the cobs, the rest of us prepared cold water for cooling and more cleaning. Mom had kept the double metal wash tubs from the old wringer washer she had used before getting an electric washing machine. It stood off the ground on three-foot legs and was easy to use. Putting the hose in the tub, we filled it with water. This would be the first step in cooling the hot ears of corn.

Filling the tubs

Dad and Newt carried the cobs over to the first tub. After a few minutes of cooling we moved them to the second tub of cold water, where we pulled off the remaining silk. Mom believed we could get it all off. I tried but rarely succeeded to do so.

After the cooling process, we were ready for the last task. We carried laundry baskets of cooked, cleaned corn to our downstairs kitchen. Here the corn would be cut off the cob, bagged, and put in the freezer for the winter. I wanted the job of cutting the corn off the cob because we did it inside where there was air conditioning. But the assignment to cut corn off the cob was not about letting a person cool off inside. It was about who would do the best job at getting all the corn cut off. Unfortunately, that person was not me, it was Newt. Working outside most of the time, he probably didn't care as much about going inside to cool off. But he cared about doing a good job with the corn.

After the corn was husked, cooked, cooled, cut, and bagged, our job was done. Preparing food like this for ourselves was much more satisfying than going to the grocery store in town and buying several cases of canned or bags of frozen corn. And the store-bought corn could not compare to our own harvest. Every time we pulled out a bag of frozen corn in the winter, I fondly remembered the summer day when we all worked together to prepare this produce that graced our family table.

Even though I often complained about the job, it was good for me to work with others as a team. Corn day provided me with the experience of being a member of this family, contributing to our common good, and enjoying the fun. Helping prepare and store food for our family was a new skill to learn, one I would do with my own children years later.

I fantasized about taking these kinds of skills back to Josephine. In my fantasy, David Cassidy took us both to California (what's the point of having a fantasy if you can't have a rock star in it). The trip would tear Josephine away from the abusive men in her life, and I would show her how to save money by growing food in our own garden rather than buying it at the store.

I didn't learn these kinds of skills living with Josephine. With Josephine, I lived in an atmosphere of lack—lack of safety, money, and food. Ultimately, I thought, it came down to a lack of skill. Josephine and her people may have blustered about being tough and having power, but they really didn't. Because of their alcoholism and poverty mindset, they had little control in the world. Their addictions and poverty had beaten them down, so they griped and blamed everyone else for their hardships.

My new family modeled a different way and attitude. I could learn to do things. Even though the work was long and we all got tired, many hands made lighter work. Yes, Dad and sometimes Mom were ill-tempered and grumpy, but they had a purpose in their judgment. Dad wanted us to do a good job and be good stewards of the harvest. His harsh judgment, though uncomfortable, was his way of helping us learn to do a good job.

That night, with the corn packed in the freezer, I lay in bed, bone tired and barely able to eke out my nightly prayers, but I felt safe and happy. I knew no one would come in my room to hurt me, which, even after multiple years with my new family, I did not take for granted. The day had been long, but the result was good. And I had been part of that good result. We had collected enough bags of corn to feed ourselves and the families of my older siblings. This sense of plenty for all was a substantial part of my gratefulness.

A deeper, unseen reality washed over me, too. I had experienced what it meant to enjoy being with a group and having fun working together. Bittersweet feelings also crept into my heart. I realized that the acquisition of new skills furthered the divide between my new life and the one with Josephine. Becoming part of my new family meant that I was losing my old family. In my old life, I learned to be helpless and rely on others. Now I was learning I could do things that really made a difference. Even though this birthing into my new family ultimately brought healing, it first brought growing pains.

"Thank you, God, for Mom and Dad," I whispered as I closed my eyes and snuggled down into a new safety and a new sense of belonging and responsibility.

Chapter 14

Fifteen and Flying Free

"Kathy, come inside for a minute."

I let out a big sigh as I turned away from my friends to the sound of Mom's voice. The talk about boys and who was going with whom stopped as the other girls became silent, too.

"Come inside, Kathy," she said for a second time. My face scrunched up as I silently questioned why she was calling me in.

This was my birthday party. We were all waiting to go to Lincoln and eat pizza at Valentino's. I wanted to get in the car, not go back into the house. Mom's face looked just as frustrated as I felt. She motioned with her hand. I walked from outside into the living room, where Mom and Dad stood close together, hiding something behind them. As I walked up to them, they moved out of the way. There it sat, just what I wanted, a Monterey bike. It had a green metal body and a soft white leather seat.

"Thanks, Mom and Dad!" I exclaimed as I hugged

them. My ear-to-ear smile said it all. I ran my hand over the leather seat and noticed its hand brakes. No more having to brake with my feet. But when I looked at the handlebars, I felt a little twinge of sadness. "You couldn't find a ten-speed with the wrap-under handlebars?" I asked, looking at Dad.

"No, the man at the shop said a three-speed would be better on these gravel roads. And those handlebars aren't good for your back. These are much better".

I wasn't convinced that a three-speed was the best choice. I suspected Dad had just bought what he thought I should have and not what I wanted. But I soon found out it was a good bike for the country roads. And when I later got a ten-speed, I didn't like the low handlebars. This bike was actually perfect for me, and I ended up loving it.

"Get on it and take it for a ride," Dad said.

I walked it out of the house and rode it down our long lane to the mailbox and back again. Then some of my friends took a turn before we left for Lincoln.

I don't remember every birthday I spent with Mom and Dad. But if we were at home, I usually had a slumber party. This bike birthday was the best one. And all the birthdays I spent with my new family had to be better than the ones with Josephine. My biological family always remembered my birthday, but I remember none of them. We probably celebrated by doing what Josephine wanted to do–going out to eat or to a bar. I didn't have childhood friends other than my cousins, so having a kids' party never happened.

Birthdays with my new family were different. The bike for my fifteenth birthday was the best present I had ever received up to then. This bike replaced the old black one I had discovered in the garage and taught myself to ride when I first came to live with the folks. Mom and Dad saw how much I rode that old bike, so they knew I would love this new one.

I rode that green bike many times to get away by myself, wandering the country roads close to our farm. One of my favorite places to ride was on the bridge that crossed over the interstate. I used to stand on the bridge and watch cars pass under me, imagining where they might be traveling. Some were going only a short distance, but I imagined others taking long trips to nearby states, maybe all the way to the East or West coasts. As a teenager, I longed to just hop in the car and travel. But for now, this bike was how I could get away by myself.

In a few short years, I would get into a car and drive to another state for college. But for the moment, this bike gave me a taste of freedom. Until then, I appreciated that I still had a few years left with Mom and Dad and the safety of my home and church.

Chapter 15

Formed and Transformed

Loud voices came from the MYF (Mennonite Youth Fellowship) room. I walked down the stairs and into the room with its familiar smells—girls' perfume and boys' body odor. The boys jumped on each other and tossed pillows back and forth. I chatted with Charnelle and Brenda as we made plans to go to Dairy Queen after MYF.

A young, newly married couple, Sid and Peg, were our youth leaders. The soft strumming of Sid's guitar beckoned us to listen above the din of the boys. Peg attempted to shush them by raising her voice. "Okay everyone, it's time to get started."

Some of the boys paused their game, but it wasn't until Michelle admonished her brother to be quiet and sit down that everyone listened. Sid and Peg were close enough to our age to be cool. I always felt safe with them. As strong Christian role models, they also helped me develop faith.

This evening, we sang several songs, including "Peace Like a River" and "Unity," two of my favorites. After singing, the Bible study began. Sid announced that the Scripture passage for the evening was 1 Corinthians 4. We took turns reading, then Sid and Peg gave us a list of questions. We discussed these questions, and were encouraged to dig deeper into our thoughts and feelings about this Scripture and how God was working in our lives.

Being in MYF was one of the best parts of my youth. Walking into the church and down to the basement youth room was like coming home. These were my people, my peers. The MYF room, decorated by our group with Bible verses on the walls beside a rainbow, was a healing place. It provided a physical structure that housed the cocoon of safety I felt with the group. This was also a place of transformation. Many things in my new life changed me, but MYF was one of the most important. In MYF I didn't feel the need to pretend everything was fine. I could just be me.

Study and discussion of the Bible helped shape my new identity. This is what I craved. Juggling the identity of being a part of my biological family and my foster family was always stressful. But being a part of this group, which represented God's family, surpassed everything else. These Bible studies gave me a playbook I could understand. Little did I know that a new seed was sprouting from the ash heap of my first ten years of life. Hope and resiliency were being pumped into my soul. I learned to be thankful, to look for a positive example to follow, and to use prayer to make a difference in my life and the world.

At church there was something more powerful that could protect me: God. This helped counter the abuse and violence I suffered in my biological family. As a follower of Jesus, I could be more than my past.

But this beautiful bubble of love and safety would soon change. The seniors, Michelle, Charnelle, and Brenda, would soon leave for Hesston College. Their departure would be a significant loss for me. I felt closer to these few people than anyone else in my life. They helped me a lot, especially Brenda. What would I do without her?

We ended with prayer and walked into the cool summer evening. Charnelle, Brenda, and I headed to DQ for some ice cream. As we sat at a table in the small building, I struggled to hold back my tears.

"What's the matter, Kathy?" Brenda asked.

"I'll miss you guys next year."

"I know, we'll miss you, too," Charnelle said.

Brenda chimed in, "You can come and visit us. You're coming for Prospective Students weekend over Thanksgiving, aren't you?"

"Yes, I'm coming," I said as I reached for another tissue in my purse.

"And we'll come home a lot, too," Charnelle said.

"Then next year you'll come to Hesston and go to school with us," Brenda said. "That will really be fun."

Talking about this quelled my loneliness and excited me. I knew I needed to look at the good, rather than the negative in my life. I felt God had blessed me so much that I shouldn't dwell on what was wrong. This perspective encouraged me.

Navigating rough waters at home and school did not feel as safe as the church. I don't remember being excluded from anything at church, but school was different. In contrast to church, high school was a competitive rat race. When a child feels like damaged goods, it's easy for them to fall to the bottom of the social hierarchy. This was the overall feeling I had at school. However, there were many good moments when I felt valued and loved by my friends. We had fun slumber parties and important talks about our teenage lives. For my 16th birthday, these same friends had a special flowerpot made for me. They knew I loved plants and gardening, so this flowerpot was a special gift.

At school, I hung out with the smart crowd, but I was never popular. The primary way I fit in was to work hard academically. That was something I could control. Being a smart, virtuous girl was my identity. But this didn't get me any dates. I wanted to go on dates, but nobody wanted me. I had many schoolgirl crushes, however, and wrote volumes of poems on this topic.

I dated one older boy for a month in high school. He went to the technical college in Milford. That's where the "bad boys" went to school. I met him through a friend. We dated hot and heavy for a month during the winter of my senior year. My parents were in Phoenix and I hadn't told them I was dating him. But they discovered I had been with this guy at a football game in his car with steamy windows. They forbade me to see him. I did what they asked and broke up with him.

Sexual attraction and desire are a normal part of development. This is how God made our bodies. But this development is skewed when a child has been sexually abused. Sexual abuse of children laces them with shame and a sense they are worthless. Sexual abuse invades the body and permeates the soul. Some teenagers deal with this by being overly sexual, but that was not how I handled it. I believed that disobeying the church's teachings on purity and my parent's rules would prove I didn't belong. Engaging with my nascent sexuality would be another reason for them to send me away.

The tension between wanting love and believing it could lead to my exclusion from my family and community pulled me in opposing directions. The reality that none of the "good" boys from church or school wanted to date me reinforced my feelings of not belonging, of being different. If anyone knew of my sexual desires, they might think I was like Josephine. This was the identity I wanted to avoid at all costs.

Chapter 16

Serving and Working

When Brenda, Charnelle, and Michelle went to Hesston College, I was left behind with a small youth group of mostly younger boys. The emptiness I felt was filled somewhat with fun and service-oriented MYF activities. That fall, we began a Helping Hands project. The bulletin announcement said youth group members would do any needed work in people's homes and then donate all money raised to Mennonite Central Committee. We didn't get many takers, but I remember raking leaves one day after school for Mary, a beloved older woman from our congregation.

The last bell rang, signaling the end of school for the day. After changing my clothes, I walked to Mary's. She lived two blocks from the school in a small, older home on a corner lot facing Main Street. The short walk in the fresh air, surrounded by beautiful red, yellow, and orange fall leaves, helped me relax from a hectic day at school.

I arrived at Mary's house before the others in my group.

"Hello, Kathy. Thanks for coming," Mary said after opening her door. "Let me get my coat, and I'll show you where the rakes are."

Mary S

By the time Mary returned, the other youth had arrived. Mary showed us where to find the rakes and metal garbage cans to put the leaves in. She went back into the house, and we started working.

After we'd raked for an hour, Mary came to the door and said, "Do you want to take a break? I've got cookies and tea."

Immediately we laid down the rakes and went inside, glad for the break and the snack. Mary chatted happily with us, asking us about school and church.

By the time we finished the snack, it was getting dark. The leaves were already raked into piles, so we put them in the back of a pickup one of the boys had brought. He offered to take the leaves out to his family's farm and burn them. Saying goodbye to Mary, we all headed home.

Paid work enabled me to plug into the community as well. When I was a freshman in high school, I worked as a dishwasher at the local café one night a week. A year later I moved up to being a waitress, a position I held for the next three years. When I came home from my first year of college, they promoted me to cook, my last task before I ended my employment there.

The owner of the café was Claridy, my former GMSA leader. She was a wonderful, positive boss. Many entertaining people came into the café, including a large cadre of local regulars who showed up every day. One such daily regular was a bachelor named Dick, though we called him Dirty Dick. Not because he was creepy, but because he was smelly and filthy. He behaved oddly and tried to joke with the waitresses. He was probably just a lonely guy who went to the café for the company. I wasn't afraid of him, but I never wanted to be alone with him.

There was a couple who were regulars, too. They ordered the same thing every time they came in. I made a game out of waiting on them by writing out their order before I went to the table. I then pretended I was writing when they said what they wanted.

I enjoyed working at the café a lot. Besides serving the food, I tried to make my customers smile. My hope was they would leave the café with their stomachs full and their spirits lighter.

Chapter 17

The Loving Care of a Smile

The neglect during my first ten years of life—physical as well as emotional—continued to plague me in my new life. Even though Josephine most likely got me immunized, her personal chaos led her to neglect keeping records of my shots. This resulted in having all my vaccines repeated when I went to live with the folks. The exception to this was the small pox vaccine, which in the 1960s was given in the arm and left a circular scar.

My teeth also needed attention. When I lived with my biological family, we often frequented bars. My brother and I had bottles of pop while Josephine and Frank drank beer. All that sugar filled my teeth with cavities. I was eight years old when I went to the dentist for the first time. They pulled four rotting molars, which left spaces in my mouth. Before these teeth were removed, I could feel jagged edges of the rotting teeth with my tongue.

When I went to live with the folks, I spent a lot of time in the office of Doc Peters, the dentist in Milford, who also went to our church. Even with the removal of my molars, most of my other teeth still needed fillings. I was always anxious when I had to go to the dentist. At Cedars, I'd been given Valium when I went to the dentist. I didn't need the Valium anymore, but it was still scary.

Some teeth turned dark because their roots had died. Two of the front teeth were gray and crooked. Before I went to college, my folks, Doc Peters, and I decided what we should do about my dental work. As the expert, Doc Peters laid out our options. Braces would straighten the teeth, but two front teeth would still be gray. There were no veneers to put on teeth, and even if there were, that option would have been too expensive. The other option was to put "caps"–now called crowns–on the three front teeth. That way, all my front teeth would be straight and white. My choice was the caps. I didn't want braces. Mom and Dad agreed, and we started the two-step process.

First Doc Peters had to grind down the old teeth and put on temporary caps. A couple weeks later, I received the permanent caps. Mom and Dad both went with me to the appointments, which signified this was a big deal. Their presence comforted me as I sat in the chair, and Doc Peters numbed my month with a big needle. I waited for the shots to take effect.

Soon Doc drilled, which was loud and jarring. This was the worst part.

When my three front teeth were ground down to make room for the caps, Doc stepped out to get the temporaries he made earlier. While he was gone, Mom and Dad, both wanted to see what my teeth now looked like. I opened my mouth, and they peered in. They asked me if I wanted a mirror. No thanks. I had no desire to see how deformed my teeth looked.

Soon Doc Peters came back to put on the temporaries. These looked okay, but the real change came when I got the permanent caps. When I first looked at them in the mirror, a big smile spread across my face. I looked good. Now I could smile with confidence.

Doc Peters did an excellent job with these caps because they lasted 40 years. I recently got the old caps replaced with new ones. The new round of dental visits produced new waves of anxiety, but also, unexpectedly, grief. I was losing a part of me I had lived with for four decades. As I recalled the experience of having the caps put on at age 17, it symbolized the care my parents had for me. They not only provided for my basic dental needs but went beyond, to give me a beautiful smile. This smile would give me more confidence when I went off to Hesston College.

As I sat in my current dentist chair—Doc Friesen working in my mouth rather than Doc Peters—I was overcome with emotion. Tears rolled down my cheeks that had nothing to do with the drilling jarring my head. Last time Mom and Dad had been with me. Now they were both gone, and I missed them. Along with the sadness came gratitude for all they had given me. They gave this terrified, broken little girl a foundation built on love and faith from which she could launch into the adult world.

Chapter 18

Graduating from Childhood

It was the middle of May 1978, and I didn't have to go to school all week. High school was over. Baccalaureate had been held on Sunday, and tonight was graduation. I was ready to leave high school and childhood, but I was sad about leaving Mom and Dad. I knew I would miss them. But going to Hesston College would be fantastic. There I would finally reunite with my good friends, Brenda, Charnelle, and Melody.

I cleaned the house, made brownies, and helped Mom make ice cream. Church people would come over after the graduation. It would be nice to have them come to my graduation party. I felt a little sad no family was coming from Kansas, but I knew they were busy, and it's difficult to take off in the midweek. Loree, who worked a full-time job in Phoenix, could not come, but she sent a neat graduation package with many cool and funny things, including a huge novelty pencil. She wrote on the accompanying card that the oversized pencil was for writing all my big ideas.

After lunch, Mom left to buy groceries in Seward for the evening festivities, and I cleaned up the dishes. I looked out the kitchen window as a green station wagon drove into the yard. At first, I wondered who it belonged to. Then the car registered in my mind–Janet's car. I dried my soapy hands on a towel and stepped into the hall leading into the back porch. The back door opened, and Jody, Cindy, and Vicki burst into the house.

They ran to me, and the three of us hugged all at once.

"What are you guys doing here?" I asked.

"We came for your graduation," Cindy said.

"Mom made a cake, and we brought decorations," Vicki said. She threw her arms out, and I reached down to hug her.

As Janet came in, she said, "Happy graduation!"

"Thanks for coming. I'm so glad you're here," I said, feeling overwhelmed.

We worked for the rest of the day before we got ready for the graduation. I was nervous. What if I tripped and fell as I walked up to get my diploma? What if I forgot to turn my tassel over? These fears ran in my head like a hamster on a wheel. But thankfully, the night flowed without a hitch.

Walking out of the Milford High School into the warm May evening, I felt freedom and relief. Soon I would move on to Hesston College. For the first time, I was shedding my old Shorny skin completely and gaining my new Burkey skin. This was who I wanted to be.

I had fun at the evening party, although I felt awkward being the center of attention. I opened my gifts in front of everyone, which also made me feel uncomfortable. What if I did something stupid and embarrassed Mom and Dad as everyone was looking at me? The guests were mainly church people, youth group leaders, and friends of my parents.

For years Mom kept a journal. This is what she wrote on my graduation day:

> *A big day—I went to Milford for groceries–had to go to both stores—picked up Ag's ice cream freezer. Come home and made ice cream 5 freezers full. Kathy made brownies and cleaned—men ate up at Shelley's (local café) because we had so much to do. After dinner, I went to Seward to pick up Kathy's luggage (my graduation gift from Mom and Dad) and a few other things. Jan and girls came about as soon as I was gone. Then Jan went to Seward, I met her on the way home. She brought a lovely decorated cake for Kathy's grad. We all worked like crazy to get done—Jan decorated the table and had to get her girls ready and herself. Take Kathy's pictures. I made sandwiches before we went.*
>
> *We had around 37 people here after–quite a conglomeration. But it worked out o.k. nice gifts and the whole bit sure did appreciate Jan–Jody–Cindy, and Vicki being here.*
>
> *Erma Burkey May 16, 1978*

Chapter 19

Beyond Milford

After high school graduation, I continued to work at the café during the summer. My body was still in Milford, but my mind had already departed for Hesston. Many of my friends were already there. Paulene and John, my siblings, also lived in Hesston and worked at the college.

The biggest thing that happened during the summer was that Mom, Dad, and I decided to change my name to Burkey. I had wanted to do this for a while, and the change was another advantage my folks could give me before I left home. There wasn't much to it. Mom and Dad contacted their lawyer, and he took it from there. But the difference this name change made in my life was enormous. Now telling people who I was, meant I wouldn't have to explain anything. I could say John was my brother or I was Paulene's sister and not have to go through the conversation of not being their "real" biological sister.

Also, Burkey is a Mennonite name. To those who are non-Mennonite, this may not seem like a big deal, but it is in this religious tradition. Mennonites have the "Mennonite game." They play this game when they meet a new person and want to understand that person's background. If you think they're Mennonite because of their last name, you ask them the names of their parents or grandparents. You also ask where they're from and what school or college they went to. This is a way to connect with people and see what things you may have in common. Also, if they give you the right "Mennonite connected" answers, you know they're in your group. With a name like Shorny, I would have been out, but a name like Burkey meant I was in.

Kathy before leaving for Hesston

With my new Mennonite name, new teeth, and my bags packed, I headed south to Kansas in late August 1978. Hesston College was a wonderful experience for me. I found many good friends, and I even dated. This move, away from home, allowed me to spread my wings while remaining in a familiar, safe place.

I also got to spend more time with my sister Paulene. She worked in the college cafeteria, and I saw her almost every day. She invited me to her house to do my wash and just hang out. In childhood, I had spent more time with Janet and her family. Now I was getting to know Paulene and her family better.

Soon after I arrived in Hesston, Paulene took me to Newton, a larger town close to Hesston, to do something forbidden. We went to Moffett's Jewelry store, and I got my ears pierced. This was something I wanted for a long time, but Dad would not allow it. With Paulene's support and encouragement, I did it anyway.

While at Hesston I also spent time at my brother John's house and babysat my young nephew, Jeremy. I also got to know Brenda, my sister-in-law, better.

With these changes and my fresh start at college, I could push the life I had with my biological family down even further. Whenever anyone asked where I was from, I said I grew up on a farm in Nebraska. I talked about Lincoln and my biological family only with my closest friends.

Most communication with Pat and Josephine had stopped. Not wanting them to know where I was, I didn't tell them about moving to Hesston. The only contact during the last years of high school and into college was at Christmas. But by the time I was a sophomore at Hesston, all communication with them had basically ended. My last conversation with Josephine occurred one night in December 1979. I was home for Christmas break.

Dad and I were sitting in the living room watching TV. Mom was reading the newspaper. We all heard the phone ring, but Mom answered it. As soon as she began

Erma and Floyd, Christmas 1979

talking, I could tell something was wrong. The pleasant expression on her face went flat. Her eyes glared as she pinched her mouth shut. I didn't think she was angry with me, but something was definitely wrong.

Taking the phone from her ear, she pointed it toward me. "It's for you, "she said in a flat tone.

Then she gave Dad a quick look. None of their emotions and interactions went past me. I was a master at reading the feelings of others. This was one way I had kept myself safe as a child.

Dad caught her look and immediately pointed the remote to the TV to mute it. This was also a signal he had a concern about the call. If it had been a friend or someone from church, Dad wouldn't interrupt his TV watching but would tell me to go to the den to take the call. Muting the TV meant he would listen in on this call. I got up and took the phone from Mom, and she took my place on the couch.

The call was from Josephine, and she was drunk. During the conversation, she asked me if I wanted to call her husband "Marvin" or "Daddy Marvin." This was a question she had asked me years earlier when she came to court. I didn't know why she was obsessed with this question. The first time she'd asked it, years earlier, I had felt saddened that she hadn't fought for me in court and didn't seem to care how I was doing. Now, as a young woman, this question frustrated and outraged me. I had moved on in my life. I was a different person from the little girl she'd left behind. I had done so much with my life, but she couldn't see any of it. Alcohol continued to control her. When she asked me this idiotic question, I had finally had enough.

Standing my ground, I said, "I have someone here I call Dad."

"Do you consider them your parents more than me?" she asked.

"Yes, I do," I answered. Then tears streamed down my face as my body shook. I don't remember Josephine's response, I stood there and cried.

Dad, who was sitting in his recliner in the living room, listening and watching, came over and took the phone from my hand. He hung it up and engulfed me in a hug. I cried in his arms. We had crossed a line that day, and I would never go back. At that point, all contact with Josephine and Pat stopped for many years.

Three months later, when I was home for spring break, Mom and Dad had a surprise. They asked me to sit at the kitchen table, saying they wanted to talk about something. Not knowing if this was good or bad, I braced myself emotionally. However, the conversation was about something fantastic.

"We've been talking to the rest of the kids about this and were wondering if you wanted to be legally adopted?" Dad said.

A huge smile spread across my face as I looked from Mom to Dad. "Really?" I said.

They both nodded yes.

"Yes, yes, that would be great," I said.

"Okay, we'll talk to the lawyer and get the process started," Dad said.

Sadly, nothing ever happened with this. I asked Dad about it a few months later, and he said because I was an adult I couldn't be legally adopted. This was disappointing for me, but I was glad they had at least tried.

Years later I heard about adults being adopted, and I wondered why my parents hadn't done this. Maybe the laws in Nebraska were different, and that was the reason. Another explanation could be that when they talked to the lawyer and heard the cost for this, they probably thought it was a better idea to save their money. The reality was I was already a part of the family, and my name was now Burkey. Spending several thousands of dollars just to have a piece of paper to make it legal probably wasn't worth it for these practical, thrifty Mennonites.

***

I graduated from Hesston College in the spring of 1980, receiving an associate's degree in early childhood education. Not knowing what to do next, I rented a house in Hesston with my roommate and worked for that summer and the next semester. In the winter, I took classes at Bethel College in North Newton, Kansas, and graduated with a degree in elementary education a year and a half later.

Continuing to follow the Mennonite path, I went into Mennonite Voluntary Service (MVS) in St. Louis. I lived in a house with five other volunteers. My service assignment was at the International Institute, working with refugees. With a newly minted teaching degree, I spent my mornings running the preschool there, for the refugee children to attend while their parents went to English classes. In the afternoons I became a social worker, visiting refugee clients in their homes or taking them to appointments around town.

My time in St Louis transformed me. It introduced me to a new life while staying in the Mennonite world. The unit was more liberal than I was used to in Milford or at Hesston. They emphasized social justice as a way of serving. Mom and Dad served God through mission work, but this more human-centered mission work involved identifying a person's physical and spiritual needs and filling those. In short, MVS introduced me to social justice. Social justice recognizes how people are treated. It works to change the culture when individuals, usually those without power and privilege, are being mistreated.

Through MVS I also had the opportunity to learn about other cultures and religions. Many of the refugees I worked with were Muslims from Afghanistan. Sadly, I didn't take the opportunity to get to know more about their religion. Because of my conservative upbringing and my desire to be accepted by Mom and Dad, I feared learning about other religions. I worried it might make me turn away from my Christian faith.

This fear of other religions became magnified during an activity for the whole MVS unit. Each month a different member of the unit got to choose an activity for everyone. This was something fun to do and a way to bring us closer as a group. This time we all went to a Hare Krishna restaurant.

When we entered the building, there was a small room, just off the entrance, with a statue of the Buddha prominently displayed as well as incense, candles and other colorful objects. This room made me feel uncomfortable. Because this religion did not center on Jesus, I didn't feel there was any good in it. The restaurant itself was also strange. The food was vegetarian, probably vegan, although at that time I didn't know what vegan meant. At this meal, I told the rest of the unit members that this was the farthest away from Milford, Nebraska, I had ever been. And that was undoubtedly true.

Throughout these first few years after I left Milford, I could put my biological family out of my conscious mind. I felt certain they didn't know where I was, and only my close friends knew anything about my time in foster care. This was mostly good. I could develop into the person I wanted to become, free of the stigma of being a foster child. But I also didn't want to accept that I still needed to deal with the trauma of my childhood. My biological family and the trauma associated with them stayed in my subconscious and came out in other ways, such as fears, anxiety, angry outbursts, and an inability to trust people.

After MVS, I moved back to Kansas and lived in Wichita, where I got my first job working for a daycare center. Later I took a position in the Wichita School

System and worked there for three years. These were all things I wanted to do, but also things I felt I *needed* to do to win Mom and Dad's acceptance.

Even though I was an adult with a college degree and a job, I still craved the approval of my parents, especially Dad. This need for acceptance and fear of rejection caused me to allow my parents to control many of the decisions in my life.

This dynamic became clear in a phone conversation with my folks around the time my nephew Marty, Janet's son, was getting married in Pennsylvania. I wanted to drive out there with one of my good friends. But Mom and Dad thought it would best if I rode to Pennsylvania with Janet's family. My anxiety and fear of acting against their wishes came to a head in a bizarre phone conversation with Mom and Dad about this trip.

"I don't think it would be a good idea for two young girls to drive across country alone," said Dad. "You should drive out with Janet and Stan. It would be a lot safer for you and not cost so much."

My response made little immediate sense, even to me. "If I drive out to Pennsylvania with Cheryl, will you send me back to Cedars?" I asked.

There was silence on the other end of the call. "What?" Mom finally asked.

"Why would we send you back to Cedars?" Dad asked.

Their confused reaction helped me come back to reality. "Oh no, I didn't mean that. It's okay. I'll tell Cheryl I'm going with Janet."

Because I had not processed my childhood grief and abandonment, and only buried it in my subconscious, I asked this question with all seriousness. It was a statement that just came out of my mouth without me thinking about it, and it caught all of us by surprise. The question was ridiculous, but at that moment it made sense to me. Now I realize it showed my need to work through these issues. But my traumatized mind wanted them to say they would keep me no matter what I did. Even if I disobeyed them.

I continued to do things that would make Mom and Dad want to keep me. I met and became engaged to a

Kathy and Tim

fantastic Mennonite man, Tim Wiens, who is also a doctor. Surely Mom and Dad couldn't ask for more. But the two worlds, of my biological and foster/adoptive families, continued to struggle inside me. Around the time of Tim's and my wedding the issue came up again. I worried that Pat or Josephine would find out about the marriage and crash the wedding. Because of this, we only put an announcement in the Milford Times newspaper and not in the Lincoln Star.

This was a genuine fear, albeit irrational. My biological family had no real way of learning I was getting married. I had not heard from either of them since the conversation I had with Josephine at Christmas when I was a sophomore at Hesston College. But the fear was there. Thankfully, they did not crash the wedding.

Tim and I were married at Bellwood, and it was a beautiful ceremony with the support of our families and many friends.

In my relationship with Tim, I finally felt safe enough to look at my past. I first saw a therapist when Tim was in residency. I have continued with therapy off and on as issues come up from my childhood.

In 1991, Pat's wife called Mom to tell her Josephine had cervical cancer and wouldn't live long. Pat's wife called my folks in Milford because they didn't know where I lived. Tim and I, along with our daughters, traveled to Nebraska. Our girls stayed with Mom and Dad in Milford, while Tim and I went to Lincoln.

We went to Josephine's small apartment. Pat and Aunt Dona (she had been married to Josephine's brother) were also there. Tim asked a lot of good questions about my childhood with them. I felt numb during the visit. My primary emotion was fear. I was afraid Pat and Josephine would find out where we lived. I was scared they would find out Tim was a doctor and try to get money from us.

Josephine died in January 1992. Mom and I went to her funeral. Afterward, several of us went to Dona's house. During this time, Pat talked about the girl he and his friends had raped (a rape I witnessed as a ten-year-old girl). He laughed about it, saying how they had kicked her out of the car and left her naked in the street. This was when I fully realized he had not changed and was not a safe person for me to be with and especially not to have my daughters around. There was no way I would ever give him access to my children. Pat never met them. He died in 2010.

My relationship with Mom and Dad and my understanding of my place in the family have continued to get better over the years. Counseling has helped me see my life less in black and white and with more nuance. I now understand there is good and bad in everyone and in everything.

Dad mellowed more in the last couple of years of his life. Even though we never had an emotionally close relationship, I always knew he loved me. In the last couple years of his life, he could express his love and appreciation a little more.

Dad's health was declining. After one surgery, he had a profound spiritual experience where he envisioned a dove touching him in his hospital bed and then flying up to heaven. Wanting to share this experience with the congregation at Bellwood, he asked me to write something up and say it from the pulpit the next Sunday. I felt honored that he would ask me to do such an important thing for him. It showed he valued me and my skill as a writer and speaker. I wrote something up and shared it with him. I wanted to make sure it was right. But his response was, "Don't worry. I trust and know you'll say the right thing."

After Dad died in 2003, I could have more stress-free, fun times with Mom. We most enjoyed eating Valentino's pizza and Mexican food, going shopping, and spending time quilting together. In March 2013, in the last few days of Mom's life, I returned to Nebraska to be with her. We knew it was her time to go, but she was still conscious and able to speak. I drove up from Kansas to her nursing home room in Seward. I had been sitting with her for a while when she said her mouth was dry. I got her a wet washcloth. As I handed her the cloth, she said, "I don't know what I would have done without you."

My reply was that "I don't know what I would have done without you either." This was true for me, but I realized that she also valued having me as a part of her life, as her daughter. These were the last words she spoke to me. They were the last gift she gave to me, and I will always cherish that memory.

Chapter 20

A Legacy of Foster Care

In my adult life, as I worked through my childhood issues with Mom and Dad, I wondered why they had been the ones to take me in. What if another family at Bellwood had wanted me instead? Perhaps a family where I would have felt more accepted and where anger wouldn't have been an issue. But as I contemplated this, I realized that Mom and Dad were the only ones in the church who took in foster children during that time.

I received a lot of love and care from the other people at Bellwood. I'm grateful for that. But without Mom and Dad, I wouldn't have been there at all. And I wouldn't have had those wonderful relationships. These realizations helped me see that even though they were not perfect parents, as I had imagined other parents might have been, they were the right parents for me.

Because of their willingness to care for foster children, they were an example to others. This legacy has helped many other needy, abused, and neglected children. Because of our parents' example, my sister Janet and her husband Stan were foster parents for years and took in many children. Four have become members of Janet's family, and they adopted my niece Nicole as a young child. Janet's daughters, Cindy and Anissa, have also been foster parents. They have adopted two of their foster children. The ripple effect of my parents' faithfulness to God and their desire to help children has touched many lives.

Their legacy in my life has also been great. For all the losses I experienced with my biological family I have gotten them back a hundredfold. My parents took in a broken and abused 11-year-old girl. They helped her find faith, purpose, and meaning in life. I have always been God's beloved daughter, and now I am fully Floyd and Erma's beloved and grateful daughter.

Epilogue

The Mennonite church can heal, and it can also harm

My parents gave me a legacy of faith, service and mission. These are values that were reinforced through the teachings as well as the care and support I received as a child at Bellwood Mennonite Church. Families and faith communities can be a great resource to instill faith in God and belief in Jesus.

My faith had its foundation at Bellwood. I am grateful for that. My childhood faith has grown and changed over the years. This change has moved from conservative evangelicalism to liberal social justice. My views and beliefs on almost every topic within the Christian world have changed. But what I learned from my parents is that we follow the call of Jesus in our life. That call has taken me places, that as a young girl, I never thought I would go.

Currently I am involved in education on child protection/sexual abuse prevention. (See the author page for the organizations I work with.) As I wrote this book, I was continually reminded of the individuals who did not have a positive church experience. My hope is that sharing my experience at Bellwood will not cause pain to those who have been abused and betrayed by a religious institution.

Churches can be sources of great help as Bellwood was for me. But I now know they can also be sources of great pain. To those who have experienced the church as a place of pain and suffering please know I believe you and I care about what you have/are experiencing. Many individuals have left the church permanently and that is what they need to do—no one should judge them. However, I have not given up on the Mennonite church.

The harm individuals experience in the church takes many forms, but ultimately there is spiritual abuse. The definition of spiritual abuse given by Jeff VanVonderen, co-author of *The Subtle Power of Spiritual Abuse* is this "Spiritual abuse occurs when someone is treated in a way that damages them spiritually" (pg. 13). Spiritual abuse is not something that only happens in cults or very controlling conservative churches. It happens in churches all over the country and this includes Mennonite churches. In my work I see the spiritual abuse that happens to victims and survivors of sexual abuse. I have also experienced spiritual abuse from a church I formerly attended.

If you have experienced sexual or spiritual abuse and would like to visit with someone about it please contact me at katherinebwiens.com or Stephanie Krehbiel at Into Account (intoaccount.org).

Acknowledgements

I would like to thank Laurie Oswald Robinson, author of *Forever Families* and editor at Mennonite Mission Network for her wisdom and support. Laurie was my writing coach through this process. This book would not be in your hands today without the help of Laurie.

I would like to thank my initial readers: Roger Schrock, retired pastor for Church of the Brethren and CASA board member; Carolyn Holderead Heggan, Sister Care Presenter and author of *Sexual Abuse in Christian Homes and Churches*; Jon Stanton, Former director of Dove's Nest and author of *Fat: A Life Unfiltered*; and Janet Voth, foster parent. Their input helped greatly in making revisions, and their encouragement of the story gave me the courage to continue the process.

My editors, Kristen Bachman and Gordon Houser, were a great help in making my story more readable.

The encouragement of my family and friends was important. Special thanks goes to my husband Tim, whose faithful love, support and encouragement has helped me in many endeavors in my life and especially this one. My brother and sisters and sister-in-law have also supported me in this journey.

Special thanks also go to all readers of my first book, *Bars, Dumps and Other Childhood Hangouts.* Their supportive comments and desire for this next book also inspired me to continue writing.

About the Author

Katherine Burkey Wiens lives in Newton, Kansas with her husband Tim. They have two adult daughters, Terra (and Das) and Ruth (and Matt). Kathy was an early childhood educator for 28 years, teaching both children and adults.

Kathy is a Licensed Professional Counselor and Trauma Recovery Coach. Currently her practice is in trauma recovery and wellness coaching. She holds graduate degrees in Elementary Education from Wichita State University and Mental Health Counseling from Emporia State University. Kathy offers training and policy reviews to churches on child protection and sexual abuse prevention. Along with her work in churches she is Board Chair of Into Account (intoaccount.org), Witness Support Specialist for GRACE: Godly Response to Abuse in Christian Environments (netgrace.org), and is on the speakers for Dove's Nest (dovesnest.net).

Kathy's current endeavor is starting **Possibilities Healing Art Studio** in Marion, KS. The studio will offer individual and group coaching, classes on health and wellness topics, and space for other forms of expressive arts.

Find out more by visiting katherinebwiens.com.

CPSIA information can be obtained
at www.ICGtesting.com
Printed in the USA
LVHW050802200421
684992LV00017B/941